lonely planet

POCKET VANCOUVER

TOP EXPERIENCES • LOCAL LIFE

BIANCA BUJAN

Contents

Plan Your Trip 04

Welcome to Vancouver ... 04

Top Experiences ... 06

Dining Out ... 12

Bar Open ... 14

For Kids ... 16

Treasure Hunt ... 18

Show Time ... 20

Responsible Travel ... 22

Active Vancouver ... 24

Festivals ... 25

Museums & Galleries ... 26

For Free ... 27

2SLGBTQI+ ... 28

Under the Radar Vancouver ... 29

Four Perfect Days ... 30

Need to Know ... 32

Vancouver Neighborhoods ... 34

Totem poles, Stanley Park (p40)

Explore Vancouver 37

Downtown & West End 39

Gastown & Chinatown 63

Yaletown & Granville Island 79

Main Street 99

Fairview & South Granville 113

Kitsilano & University of British Columbia 129

Worth a Trip

Richmond Night Market 13

Grouse Mountain 17

Survival Guide 145

Before You Go 146

Arriving in Vancouver 147

Getting Around 148

Essential Information 150

Index 155

Special Features

Stanley Park 40

Vancouver Art Gallery 44

Capilano Suspension Bridge Park 60

Dr Sun Yat-Sen Classical Chinese Garden 64

Granville Island Public Market 80

Science World 100

VanDusen Botanical Garden 114

Museum of Anthropology 130

Welcome to Vancouver

Stunning seascapes, majestic mountains and towering trees frame this coastal city, where you can cycle, shop, ski and swim all in one day. Here, the culinary and cultural offerings are as diverse as the neighborhoods that give the city its unique charm, and a mélange of urban dwellers and outdoor daredevils add character to your surroundings, wherever you may go.

Science World (p100) and BC Place Stadium (p89)
DAN BRECKWOLDT/SHUTTERSTOCK © ARCHITECT BRUNO FRESCHI

Vancouver's Top Experiences

Cycle the Stanley Park Seawall (p40)

OLEG CHARYKOV/GETTY IMAGES ©

LISSANDRA MELO/SHUTTERSTOCK ©

Peruse paintings at the Vancouver Art Gallery (p44)

Get goodies at Granville Island Public Market (p80)

JULIEN HAUTCOEUR/SHUTTERSTOCK ©

Entertain the entire family at Science World (p100)

DAN BRECKWOLDT/SHUTTERSTOCK © ARCHITECT BRUNO FRESCHI

Teeter above the treetops at Capilano Suspension Bridge Park (p60)

LISSANDRA MELO/SHUTTERSTOCK ©

BENEDEK/GETTY IMAGES ©

Sip tea at Dr Sun Yat-Sen Classical Chinese Garden (p64)

ALENA CHARYKOVA/SHUTTERSTOCK ©

See the forest of totem poles at the Museum of Anthropology (p130)

Bask in the blooms at VanDusen Botanical Garden (p114)

STEPHANIE BRACONNIER/LONELY PLANET ©

Dining Out

DEYMOSHR/SHUTTERSTOCK ©

Global cuisine is a highlight here, with award-winning chefs serving up flavors from around the world. Fresh-catch seafood shines, and locally sourced farm-to-table food has put Vancouver on the Michelin map. From fine-dining feasts to good-value street eats, follow your taste buds on a culinary journey through the best of the city.

Seafood City

When you can see the ocean from your seat you know your seafood is fresh. In Vancouver, local salmon, halibut, spot prawns and freshly shucked oysters are plentiful. Fresh-off-the-boat fish feeds the thriving sushi scene, and even grab-and-go fish and chips satisfies here.

Seafood fans should start with a visit to Granville Island, where the public market (pictured left) showcases some of the city's best seafood vendors, and Fisherman's Wharf sells seafood along the Stanley Park Seawall.

Global Cuisine

A beautiful blend of cultures is found in Vancouver, and this mix is reflected in the city's diverse restaurant scene.

Vancouver boasts the best Asian cuisine found outside of Asia, thanks to an influx of immigrants from the region. Authentic foods from South America to Southeast Asia can be found throughout the city.

Street Eats

Michelin may have recognized the fine-dining food scene in Vancouver this year, but the streetside vendors and off-road, mom-and-pop shops are equally notable.

Start with a trip to Vancouver's downtown food trucks, where everything from tacos to Thai food can be enjoyed curbside.

For the best on offer, check out streetfoodapp.com/vancouver.

RONNIE CHUA/SHUTTERSTOCK ©

Best Fine Dining

St Lawrence Restaurant Elevated French cuisine in a laid-back lounge. (p73)

Tojo's Legendary *omakase* (personalized chef) experience combining traditional Japanese with a 'Tojo twist.' (p122)

Boulevard Kitchen & Oyster Bar A sophisticated showcase of West Coast seafood with an international influence. (p53)

Best Global Cuisine

Anh & Chi Contemporary Vietnamese restaurant loved by hungry locals. (p104)

Sula Indian Restaurant Top-notch South Indian cuisine with a stellar cocktail list. (p105)

Yasma Flavorful Syrian-Lebanese fare in a stunning waterfront setting. (p53)

Best Street Foods

Tacofino Taco Bar Food truck turned street-food eatery featuring a West Coast take on Mexican classics. (p70)

Japadog Iconic Japanese-style hot dogs served up streetside. (p53)

Worth a Trip: Richmond Night Market

Only 20 minutes by car from Vancouver, Richmond Night Market (pictured right) is home to the largest population of Chinese residents outside of Asia, and its food scene showcases the best cuisine from the region. Take your taste buds on a round-the-world journey with a visit to Richmond Night Market – the largest outdoor market in North America. Foodies flock here to dine on dishes from the 110-plus food trucks serving up 600 bites and bevies from Asia and around the world.

Bar Open

Backroad breweries, Michelin-recognized mixology, and urban winemaking make up the diverse drinking scene in Vancouver. Grab a pint at one of Gastown's gastropubs, sip a craft cocktail at one of North America's top bars found downtown, or hit a waterfront patio for dinner and drinks with family or friends.

ROY LANGSTAFF/ALAMY STOCK PHOTO ©

Canadian Cocktails

Innovative cocktails that incorporate BC-made spirits are a must-try in Vancouver, and the options are plentiful here.

The emerging mocktails scene is also notable, where hot spots are serving up spirit-free sips without sacrificing flavor (and best of all – leaving you hangover-free).

Local Wine

British Columbia has a budding wine scene, with a variety of grapes grown at the more than 300 vineyards that range from the Fraser Valley (one hour from Vancouver) to the Okanagan Valley (five hours from the city).

As a result, exceptional, award-winning wines of all varieties are attracting global attention.

Craft Beer

As one of Canada's craft-beer capitals, Vancouver has dozens of producers to discover, and many of their beers can be found on tap wherever you dine.

For a tasting tour of the best beer in town, consider a craft-brewery crawl through Main St, or the Commercial Dr 'Yeast Vancouver' Ale Trail. For more on the best local beer spots, visit bcaletrail.ca.

Best Beer Bars

Alibi Room Vancouver's fave craft-beer tavern, with around 50 mostly BC drafts. (pictured left; p74)

33 Acres Brewing Microbrewery with modern decor, serving up craft beer and hearty snacks. (p106)

Brassneck Brewery Chill craft brewery with a small, wood-lined tasting room. (p105)

JOHN MITCHELL/ALAMY STOCK PHOTO ©

Best Happy Hours

Liberty Distillery 3pm to 6pm Monday to Thursday. (pictured right; p91)

Uva Wine & Cocktail Bar 2pm to 5pm daily. (p55)

Keefer Bar 5pm to 7pm Sunday to Friday. (p75)

Sing Sing Beer Bar 3pm to 6pm daily. (p107)

Best Cocktail Joints

Botanist Vancouver's top cocktail bar serves up sophisticated sips with a twist. (p55)

Shameful Tiki Room A windowless tiki-themed cave with some strong concoctions. (p106)

Keefer Bar Chinatown's fave lounge, with great drinks and a cool-ass vibe. (p75)

Best Bar Patios

Tap & Barrel Bridges Behemoth patio with breathtaking water and city views. (p105)

Narrow Lounge Tiny 'secret garden' back area with intimate party vibe. (p107)

Lift Bar & Grill Rooftop bar with stunning Stanley Park views. (p54)

Best Bars for Food

Alibi Room Hearty elevated comfort food and an excellent beer list. (p74)

Caffe Barney Cheerful bar and bustling brunch spot loved by locals. (p123)

Lift Bar & Grill Pair snacks with scenic Stanley Park views and great brews. (p54)

For Kids

Family-friendly Vancouver is stuffed with activities and attractions for kids, including interactive science centers, animal encounters and plenty of outdoor activities to tire them out before bed. Several festivals are especially kid-tastic, and local transport experiences, including SeaBus and SkyTrain, are highlights for many youngsters.

JEFF WHYTE/SHUTTERSTOCK ©

Wild Side of City Life

As a city surrounded by nature, Vancouver offers a wealth of outdoor adventures and wild critters both within its limits and an easy distance away.

Parks and playgrounds are plentiful, many within a short walk of downtown, and local gardens, nearby mountains and a world-renowned aquarium satisfy little ones looking for a walk on the wild side.

Satisfying Curious Kids

Are your kids fascinated by science, enamored with animals or tempted by travel? Great news: Vancouver has many attractions that appeal to curious little ones looking to learn through play.

Best of all, many of the most attractive kid-friendly sites can be found indoors, providing fun for the whole family on a rainy day.

Best Wildlife Viewing

Bloedel Conservatory A domed paradise packed with exotic birds and butterflies. (p120)

Stanley Park Lost Lagoon Find blue herons, hummingbirds and wandering raccoons along the lagoon's perimeter pathway. (p41)

Vancouver Aquarium A marine research center that showcases wildlife from the tropics to the Arctic. (pictured right; p52)

RAINER PLENDL/SHUTTERSTOCK ©

Best Parks

Stanley Park Water parks, a public pool and four fun-filled playgrounds invite active play. (p40)

Queen Elizabeth Park Wide open spaces, gorgeous gardens and lush landscapes. (p120)

Granville Island Water Park The biggest free water park in North America, found adjacent to an expansive green park. (p89)

Best Indoor Attractions

Science World A hands-on science center packed with engaging activities. (p100)

Kids Market A three-level, kid-centric mall with an arcade, a play area, and tons of toy stores. (pictured left; p89)

HR MacMillan Space Centre Astronomy museum that makes learning about space fun for kids. (p137)

Worth a Trip: Grouse Mountain

Take a scenic gondola ride to the top of **Grouse Mountain** (grousemountain.com) on Vancouver's North Shore, where you can get up close with Coola and Grinder, a pair of orphaned grizzly bears, plus see the owls and eagles that take refuge here.

Treasure Hunt

WIRESTOCK CREATORS/SHUTTERSTOCK ©

Vancouver's retail scene has grown dramatically in recent years. Hit Robson St's mainstream chains, then discover the hip, independent shops of Gastown, Main St and Commercial Dr. Granville Island is stuffed with artsy stores and studios, while South Granville and Kitsilano's 4th Ave serve up a wide range of tempting boutiques.

Independent Fashion

From vintage to high-fashion, Vancouver has a wealth of independent shops to suit many tastes.

Watch for pop-up shops and check the pages of *Vancouver Magazine* and *Georgia Straight* for retail happenings.

If the timing's right, check out the work of local designers at Vancouver Fashion Week, a semiannual event hosted in Chinatown.

Arts & Crafts

Arts are aplenty in Vancouver, with galleries, shops and streetside displays that showcase the diversity of the city.

Granville Island is packed with creative curiosities for arts enthusiasts, and authentic Indigenous art studios provide insight into the cultural significance of the carvings, jewelry and paintings you'll see around town.

Check out gotcraft.com for upcoming arts and crafts events.

Souvenirs

Skip the smoked-salmon and maple-syrup souvenirs of yesteryear, and pick up some locally crafted keepsakes that will remind you of your Vancouver visit for years to come.

Consider Indigenous jewelry, a book on Vancouver's eye-popping history (*Sensational Vancouver* by Eve Lazarus, for example) or a quirky Vancouver-designed T-shirt from the Main St fashion stores.

JSMIMAGES/ALAMY STOCK PHOTO ©

Best Shops

Regional Assembly of Text Brilliantly creative stationery store with a little gallery nook. (pictured right; p109)

Pacific Arts Market Friendly gallery space showcasing dozens of regional creatives. (p126)

Red Cat Records Main St music-store legend. (pictured left; p109)

Best Bookstores

Paper Hound Perfectly curated, mostly used, downtown bookstore. (p57)

Massy Books Tome-lined Chinatown shop with secret bookcase nook. (p76)

Kidsbooks Giant, child-focused bookstore. (p143)

Pulpfiction Books This is Vancouver's favorite multibranch used-book store. (p111)

Best Record Shops

Red Cat Records Cool array of vinyl and CDs. (p109)

Neptoon Records Classic vinyl-focused store, perfect for browsing. (p110)

Zulu Records Giant selection in a *High Fidelity*–like setting. (p143)

Best Vintage Shopping

Mintage Mall Upstairs shared vendor space in Mount Pleasant. (p111)

Eastside Flea Find vintage clothes and crafts at this regular event. (p76)

Gore St Vintage Vancouver vintage collective in Chinatown. (p77)

Best Arts & Crafts

Pacific Arts Market Upstairs gallery lined with the work of dozens of artists and artisans. (p126)

Net Loft Collective of shops featuring handcrafted fashions, crafts and specialty goods. (p95)

Urban Source Create your own masterpiece via this beloved craft store. (p110)

Show Time

You'll never run out of options if you're looking for a good time here. Vancouver is packed with diverse activities from high- to lowbrow, perfect for those craving a play one night, a hockey game the next and a rocking poetry slam to follow. Ask the locals for tips and they'll likely point out grassroots happenings you never knew existed.

Concerts

The superstar acts typically hit the stages at sports stadiums and downtown theaters, while smaller indie bands crowd tight spaces around town.

Local record stores offer the lowdown on venues and acts to catch.

Vancouver has wide musical tastes and, with some digging, you'll find jazz, folk, classical and opera performances around the city too.

Theater

Vancouver has a long history of treading the boards. The **Arts Club Theatre Company** (artsclub.com) is the city's leading troupe, with three stages dotted around the city.

The Cultch (thecultch.com) is a small community cultural space found off Commercial Dr that showcases plays and performances for smaller audiences.

Also consider January's **PuSh Festival** (pushfestival.ca) and **Vancouver Fringe Festival** (vancouverfringe.com) in September.

Film Festivals

There are plenty of places to catch blockbusters as well as subtitled art-house movies here: check cinemaclock.com for listings.

There's also a huge range of movie festivals, including late September's giant **Vancouver International Film Festival** (viff.org) and smaller festivals such as May's **DOXA Documentary Film Festival** (doxafestival.ca) and **Vancouver**

Asian Film Festival (vaff.org) held in November.

Best Live Music Bars

Guilt & Co Subterranean bar with regular shows. (p74)

Uva Wine & Cocktail Bar Check ahead for live jazz nights. (p55)

Best Live Theater

Bard on the Beach Modern takes on Shakespeare's plays, performed in waterfront Vanier Park tents. (pictured right; p141)

Theatre Under the Stars Summertime musical performances in Stanley Park. (p56)

Stanley Theatre Historic Arts Club theater venue with great end-of-season musicals. (pictured left; p125)

Firehall Arts Centre Leading independent theater with eclectic line-up of shows. (p75)

Best Alternative Entertainment

Cinematheque This beloved art-house cinema hosts a summer film noir series. (p56)

Rickshaw Theatre Under-the-radar thrash and punk venue. (p75)

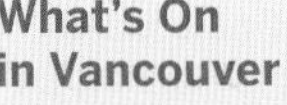

What's On in Vancouver

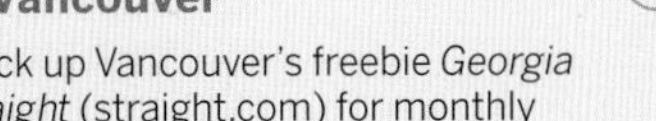

- Pick up Vancouver's freebie *Georgia Straight* (straight.com) for monthly happenings.
- Head online to Live Van (livevan.com) for up-to-the-minute local gig listings.

Responsible Travel

Positive, sustainable and feel-good experiences around the city.

ROBINOTOF/SHUTTERSTOCK ©

Leave a Small Footprint

- Use reusable water bottles and coffee mugs.
- Consider walking, cycling or using public transit to get around the city.
- Opt for sustainable and ecofriendly activities and venues.
- Buy clothes and keepsakes from local businesses and resale shops.
- Leave no trace when exploring the outdoors (take your garbage with you).

Support Local

Take a local-led walking tour through the city Park the car and opt instead for a guided walking tour, like the Gastronomic Gastown tour offered by Vancouver Foodie Tours (p82), which takes you to hidden spots and delicious dining destinations around Vancouver's oldest neighborhood.

Another option is the Talking Trees tour through Stanley Park, offered by Indigenous-owned **Talaysay Tours** (aboriginalecotours.com).

Use local businesses Skip the chain restaurants and big box stores and shop local instead. Dine at Salmon n' Bannock (p122), Vancouver's only Indigenous restaurant. Get gifts made by local designers and artisans at Granville Island's Net Loft (p95).

Pick Sustainable Venues

Book a sustainable hotel The **Fairmont Waterfront** (fairmont.com) is within walking distance of most of Vancouver's downtown attractions. The hotel is disposable free,

ANDROVER/SHUTTERSTOCK ©

offers leftover food to local charities and has carbon-neutral options in guest rooms. The hotel's sustainable rooftop garden, built in partnership with the Hives for Humanity Pollinator Corridor project, is home to thousands of honeybees.

Other downtown hotels such as the **Shangri-La** (shangri-la.com) and the **Listel Hotel Vancouver** (thelistelhotel.com) have achieved the coveted Five Green Key designation – a worldwide sustainability certification based on eco initiatives.

Visit ecofriendly venues If you're hosting an event, the **Vancouver Convention Centre** (pictured; vancouverconvention centre.com) is the world's first convention centre to have earned double LEED Platinum certification. It has the largest green roof in Canada, and is within walking distance of many ecofriendly hotels.

Vancouver Public Library (p52) is also topped with a 1850-sq-meter green roof.

Useful Resources

To find a list of Vancouver's certified sustainable hotels, visit the Green Key Global site (greenkey global.com).

Find Vancouver's most ecofriendly restaurants on EcoMeter (eco-meter.ca), a website that ranks a city's dining options based on both sustainability and community support.

Consider the pay-per-day bike-use option offered by Mobi Bike Share (mobibikes.ca), with bikes available in various locations around downtown.

Active Vancouver

EB ADVENTURE PHOTOGRAPHY/SHUTTERSTOCK ©

Vancouver's variety of outdoorsy activities is a huge hook. You can ski in the morning and hit the beach in the afternoon; hike or bike scenic forests; paddleboard the coastline; or kayak to your heart's content – and it will be content, with grand mountain views as your backdrop. There's also a full menu of spectator sports here.

Cycling & Hiking

Vancouver is a cycle-friendly city with designated routes and a bike-share scheme. For maps and resources, see vancouver.ca/cycling.

There's also an active mountain-biking scene on the North Shore; start your research via nsmba.ca.

Hiking-wise, the region is striped with cool trail treks; see vancouvertrails.com for ideas.

On the Water

It's hard to beat the joy of a sunset kayak around the coastline here. But hitting the water isn't only about paddling: there are also plenty of opportunities to surf, kiteboard and stand-up paddleboard. Several operators can take you out to sea, too.

Best Outdoor Action

Stanley Park Seawall Breathtakingly scenic walking, jogging and cycling trail. (p40)

Vancouver Water Adventures Perfect sunset paddling activity on False Creek. (p90)

Arbutus Greenway Walk, jog or bike the city's new linear park, from Kitsilano to the Fraser River. (p141)

Best Spectator Sports

Vancouver Canucks The city's fave NHL hockey passion. (p56)

Vancouver Whitecaps Vancouver's major-league soccer team. (p92)

Vancouver Canadians Nostalgic minor-league baseball fun. (p125)

Festivals

ILARIA VECCHI/SHUTTERSTOCK ©

While July and August are peak months for festivals, Vancouver has a year-round roster of events worth checking into before you arrive. Explore the websites of local listings magazines such as the Georgia Straight (straight.com) to see what's coming up.

Art & Music

Cultural festivals are hugely popular with Vancouverites, and there are stage, film and art festivals of all sizes here throughout the year. Live-music events really bring party-loving locals together, including huge annual jazz and folk events that have been running for years.

Community Events

If you truly want to connect with the locals, plan to be in the city for the July 1 **Canada Day** party, when thousands flock to Canada Pl (pictured) for live music, flag-waving and a fireworks finale.

There are also many grassroots festivals throughout the year, including colorful events staged by the Chinese, Italian, Greek and Japanese communities.

Best Art Festivals

Vancouver International Film Festival (viff.org) Huge late-September showcase of movies from Canada and around the world.

Vancouver International Jazz Festival (coastaljazz.ca) Stages around the city in June, with hundreds of live shows.

Vancouver Mural Festival (vanmuralfest.ca) A summertime street-art extravaganza that spans the Main St corridor.

Best Community Festivals

Pacific National Exhibition (pne.ca) Century-old summertime fair that lures thousands of locals.

Chinese New Year (cbavancouver.ca) Chinatown party in January or February, with a street parade included.

Car Free Day Vancouver (carfreevancouver.org) Communities across the city close their streets for live music and activities in June and July.

Museums & Galleries

While outdoor action monopolizes the spare time of many Vancouverites, there are also plenty of cultural attractions if you love rubbing your chin rather than your calves. Check to see what's on via local listings magazine the Georgia Straight (straight.com).

ALENA CHARYKOVA/SHUTTERSTOCK ©

Museums

The city's de facto museum district, Vanier Park is home to three visit-worthy institutions, including Vancouver's main history museum. A short drive away, the University of British Columbia campus houses several excellent attractions, including a natural-history museum and an anthropology-themed institution that many regard as Vancouver's best museum.

Galleries

The city's main downtown art gallery is one of the finest in Western Canada. But the city is also home to several smaller art museums as well as a healthy array of private galleries that always welcome visitors.

Check ahead for show openings and citywide art festivals.

Best Museums & Galleries

Vancouver Art Gallery The city's main gallery, combining blockbuster visiting shows and local contemporary art. (p44)

Bill Reid Gallery of Northwest Coast Art Only public gallery in Canada dedicated to contemporary Indigenous Northwest Coast art. (p50)

Museum of Vancouver Telling the story of the region via several colorful galleries. (p136)

Beaty Biodiversity Museum Natural-history museum on the UBC campus. (p136)

Engine 374 Pavilion Historic Vancouver steam locomotive, preserved in Yaletown. (pictured; p88)

For Free

FELIX LIPOV/SHUTTERSTOCK ©

There's a full array of sights and activities to enjoy in Vancouver without opening your wallet. Follow the locals and check city blogs and you'll soon be perusing art shows, noodling around parks and taking in a gratis tour or two.

Freebie Sights

You'll discover there's no need to splash the cash to have a great day out in Vancouver.

From landmark historic buildings to smaller museums and gallery spaces plus a host of parks, gardens and a couple of cool nature-themed attractions, fee-free activities are easy to find here.

Discounts Galore

The Vancouver Art Gallery offers by-donation entry on Tuesday evenings from 5pm to 9pm; and the Bill Reid Gallery of Northwest Coast Art offers free admission for all between 2pm and 5pm on the first Friday of every month.

You can also find two-for-one tickets to day-of-show events at Ticketmaster (ticketmaster.ca).

Best Free Attractions

Engine 374 Pavilion The locomotive that pulled the first transcontinental passenger train into Vancouver. (p88)

Stanley Park Nature House Fascinating introduction to the region's flora and fauna. (p51)

Marine Building This is Vancouver's favorite art-deco skyscraper. (pictured; p50)

Vancouver Public Library Rooftop Garden Elevated views of the downtown cityscape. (p52)

2SLGBTQI+

EB ADVENTURE PHOTOGRAPHY/SHUTTERSTOCK ©

Vancouver's 2SLGBTQI+ scene (2S recognizes Two-Spirit people in Canada) is part of the city's culture rather than a subsection of it. The legalization of same-sex marriage here makes it a popular spot for those who want to tie the knot in scenic style. But if you just want to kick back and have a good time, there are plenty of spots for that too.

West End

Davie Village in Vancouver's West End has a vibrant vibe centering on the 2SLGBTQI+ community, complete with pink-painted bus shelters and rainbow-striped street crossings. There's a full menu of scene-specific pubs and bars here, and it's a warm and welcoming district for everyone.

Commercial Dr in Vancouver is also a great hub for inclusive events and happenings.

Pride Week

Canada's biggest 2SLGBTQI+ celebration, Pride Week (pictured), takes place in the first week of August. It's centered on a huge parade of disco-pumping floats, drum-beating marching bands and barely clad locals dancing with boundless energy. There are also galas, drag contests, all-night parties and a popular queer film fest throughout the week.

Around the same time, East Vancouver's annual **Dyke March** (vancouverdykemarch.com) also pops up, concluding with its own festival in Grandview Park.

Best Bars & Businesses

Fountainhead Pub Laid-back, beer-friendly gay-community pub. (p55)

1181 Smooth lounge bar; great spot to see and be seen. (p56)

Little Sister's Book & Art Emporium Long-time 'gayborhood' legend, stocking books and beyond. (p57)

Under the Radar Vancouver

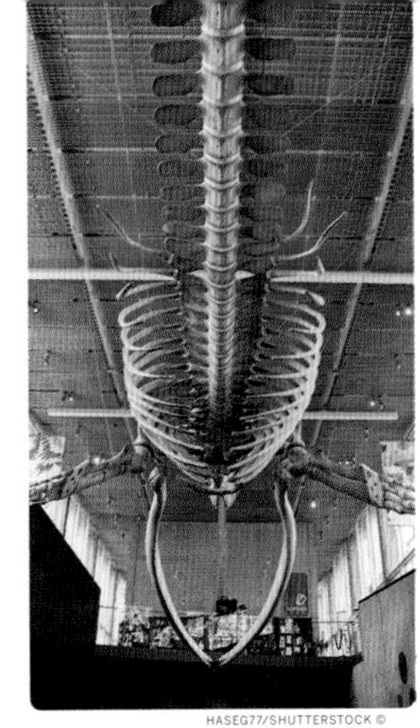

HASEG77/SHUTTERSTOCK ©

For those keen to encounter Vancouver beyond its well-known signature attractions, there are lots of walk-worthy neighborhoods, grassroots local experiences and off-the-beaten-path green spaces to discover here.

Alternative Neighborhoods

Explore the independent shops and cafes on Main St, the Victorian homes and heritage apartment buildings of the West End or the strollable storefronts and nearby beaches of Kitsilano's 4th Ave area.

From Kitsilano, add a visit to the University of British Columbia (UBC) campus. This shoreline uni offers top-notch cultural attractions that are rarely crowded – don't miss the **Beaty Biodiversity Museum** (pictured; p136).

Smaller Attractions

History buffs should visit the West End's **Roedde House Museum** (roeddehouse.org), downtown's art-deco Marine Building (p50) and Yaletown's free-entry **Engine 374 Pavilion** (p88) – home of the first transcontinental passenger train, which trundled into Vancouver in 1887.

Need a nature break? Swap Stanley Park's (p40) crowded seawall promenade for its tranquil interior trails, complete with raccoons, hummingbirds and more.

If you're near downtown's Colosseum-shaped Vancouver Public Library (p52), nip inside and visit its 'secret' rooftop garden.

Four Perfect Days

Day 1

GAGLIARDIPHOTOGRAPHY/SHUTTERSTOCK ©

Get up early and cycle around **Stanley Park** (p40). Admire the park's towering **totem poles**, and look out for Lost Lagoon and the *Girl in a Wetsuit* statue (pictured).

Make your way to **Hawksworth** (p54) for a leisurely lunch or dine alfresco at **1931 Gallery Bistro** (p45) before beginning a gallery tour through downtown.

Peruse paintings at the **Vancouver Art Gallery** (p44), and head to the **Bill Reid Gallery of Northwest Coast Art** (p50) to admire the works of the city's hailed Haida artist.

Finally, stroll and shop along Robson St, and then toast your day out with a feast and a flight of craft beer at **Forage** (p53).

Day 2

LAVINIA MAZDUL/SHUTTERSTOCK ©

Start with a stroll along the cobblestone streets of Gastown and snap a photo of the **Steam Clock** (p69) before browsing the Water St shops, including **Herschel Supply Co** (p77) and **John Fluevog Shoes** (p77).

Chinatown is right next door. Explore Vancouver's Chinese-Canadian history through immersive exhibits at the **Chinatown Storytelling Centre** (p70), then take a tour through tranquil **Dr Sun Yat-Sen Classical Chinese Garden** (pictured; p64), finishing with a cup of complimentary tea.

Fuel up with a dinner of contemporary Chinese cuisine at nearby **Sai Woo** (p71) or **Bao Bei** (p73), or if you can snag a table, head to local legend **Phnom Penh** (p70).

Day 3

MEUNIERD/SHUTTERSTOCK © ARCHITECT BRUNO FRESCHI

Start your day with a gala-vant through the city's iconic geodesic dome, **Science World** (pictured; p100). Stroll up Main St on a self-guided tour of the **Vancouver Mural Festival** (p104), with street art decorating the area's side streets.

Explore the cool boutiques around the Main St and Broadway intersection, including vintage fave **Mintage Mall** (p111) and **Turnabout Luxury Resale** (p111), and then continue up Main St to shop Vancouver's best indie stores, from vinyl-loving **Neptoon Records** (p110) to quirky **Regional Assembly of Text** (p109).

Wrap up your day with an early dinner at vibrant Vietnamese hot spot **Anh & Chi** (p104), washed down with a creative selection of tasty cocktails.

Day 4

HOWARD SANDLER/SHUTTERSTOCK ©

Bask in the blooms at **VanDusen Botanical Garden** (p114) and look for local wildlife as you meander around the mirror-calm lake. If you're feeling snacky, enjoy a coffee and treat at **Truffles cafe**. Then pop into the domed **Bloedel Conservatory** (pictured; p120) to see exotic species of birds and butterflies.

Hit the stretch of stylish shops along South Granville. Pick up some keepsakes from **Pacific Arts Market** (p126) while you're there, and take home some sweet treats from **Purdys Chocolates** (p127).

Head to Granville Island and snack your way through the **Public Market** (p80) before catching the sunset with brews and views from the **Tap & Barrel Bridges** (p92) patio.

Need to Know

For detailed information, see Survival Guide (p145)

Currency
Canadian dollar ($)

Languages
English, French

Visas
Not required for US, Commonwealth and some European visitors. Required by those from 130 other countries. Most foreign nationals flying here require a $7 Electronic Travel Authorization (eTA).

Money
ATMs are widespread. Credit cards are accepted at most businesses.

Mobile Phones
Local SIM cards may be used with some international phones. Check your provider's roaming charges.

Time
Pacific Time (GMT/UTC minus eight hours)

Tipping
Bar and restaurant tipping is routine (typically 15%).

Daily Budget

Budget: Less than $100
Dorm bed: $50

Food-court meal: $10; pizza slice: $3

Happy-hour beer special: $6

All-day transit pass: $10.25

Midrange: $100–300
Double room in a standard hotel: $200

Dinner for two in a neighborhood restaurant: $40 (excl drinks)

Craft beer for two: $15

Museum entry: $15–25

Top End: More than $300
Four-star hotel room: from $350

Fine-dining meal for two: $100

Cocktails for two: $25

Taxi trips around the city: $5 and up

Advance Planning

Three months before Book summer-season hotel stays and sought-after tickets for hot shows, festivals and live performances.

One month before Book car rental and reserve a table at a top restaurant or two. Buy tickets for Vancouver Canucks and Vancouver Whitecaps games.

One week before Check the *Georgia Straight's* online listings (straight.com) to see what local events are coming up.

Arriving in Vancouver

Vancouver International Airport

YVR is 13km from downtown. To reach the city center, hop Canada Line SkyTrain services ($8 to $10.90), take a taxi (around $35) or hire a car.

Pacific Central Station

Vancouver's long-distance train station is near the Main St-Science World SkyTrain transit station, a five-minute ride from downtown. Taxis are also available here.

BC Ferries

BC Ferries vessels from around the region dock at Tsawwassen, an hour south of Vancouver, and Horseshoe Bay, 30 minutes away in West Vancouver. Both are linked to transit bus services.

Getting Around

Bicycle

Vancouver has 300km of designated bike routes and a public bike-share scheme.

Boat

Local mini-ferries and public-transit SeaBuses navigate city waterways.

Bus

Extensive TransLink public bus services operate in Vancouver and beyond.

Train

TransLink's rapid-transit SkyTrains service local and suburban destinations.

Taxi

Several taxi companies operate here. Ride-share services are also available around the city.

EB ADVENTURE PHOTOGRAPHY/SHUTTERSTOCK ©

Vancouver Neighborhoods

Yaletown & Granville Island (p79)
On opposite sides of False Creek, these enticing areas host some of the city's best shopping and dining options.

Museum of Anthropology

Kitsilano & University of British Columbia (p129)
Beaches and heritage homes lure the locals to Kits while the nearby campus has some top day-out attractions.

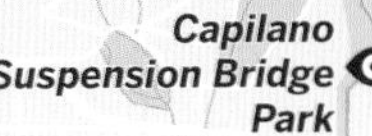

Downtown & West End (p39)
Lined with shops and restaurants, city center Vancouver adjoins the largely reidential West End plus spectacular Stanley Park.

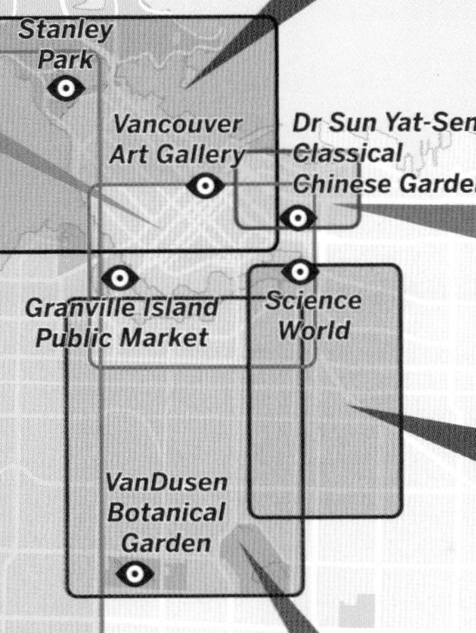

Gastown & Chinatown (p63)
Side-by-side historic neighborhoods studded with some of Vancouver's best bars, restaurants and one-of-a-kind boutiques.

Main Street (p99)
The skinny-jeaned heart of Vancouver's hipster scene houses many of its best independent cafes, shops and restaurants.

Fairview & South Granville (p113)
Twin residential areas with highly walkable shopping and dining streets plus some green attractions.

GASTOWN

Explore Vancouver

Downtown & West End 39

Gastown & Chinatown 63

Yaletown & Granville Island 79

Main Street 99

Fairview & South Granville 113

Kitsilano & University of British Columbia 129

Vancouver's Walking Tours

Downtown Grand Tour 46

Lower Lonsdale Wander 58

Chinatown Culture & History Crawl 66

Granville Island Artisan Amble 84

Commercial Drive Beer & Bites 96

South Granville Stroll 116

UBC Campus & Gardens Walk 132

Steam Clock, Gastown (p69) DANIEL AVRAM/SHUTTERSTOCK ©

Explore

Downtown & West End

The heart of Vancouver is an ocean-fringed peninsula easily divided into three: the grid-pattern city-center streets of shops, restaurants and glass towers fanning from the intersection of Granville and West Georgia Sts; the well-maintained 1950s apartment blocks and residential side streets of the West End (also home to Vancouver's gay district); and Stanley Park, Canada's finest urban green space.

The Short List

- ***Stanley Park Seawall (p50)*** *Cycling the perimeter pathway for sigh-triggering views of the forest-fringed ocean.*
- ***Marine Building (p50)*** *Spotting multiple ocean- and transport-themed motifs on the exterior of this art-deco skyscraper masterpiece.*
- ***Bill Reid Gallery of Northwest Coast Art (p50)*** *Browsing Indigenous art pieces by Haida master artist Bill Reid and others.*

Getting There & Around

Downtown's grid street system is walkable and easy to navigate.

SkyTrain's Expo Line and Canada Line both run through downtown.

Bus 5 trundles along Robson St, bus 6 along Davie St, bus 10 along Granville St and bus 19 into Stanley Park.

There are multiple car parks and parking meters here. Stanley Park has pay-and-display parking.

Downtown & West End Map on p48

Downtown (p46)

Top Experience

Cycle the Stanley Park Seawall

One of North America's largest urban green spaces, Stanley Park is revered for its dramatic forest-and-mountain oceanfront views. But there's more to this 400-hectare woodland than looks. The park is studded with nature-hugging trails, family-friendly attractions, sunset-loving beaches and tasty places to eat. There's also the occasional unexpected sight to search for (besides the raccoons that call the place home).

MAP P48, C1

vancouver.ca/parks

Seawall

Built in stages between 1917 and 1980, the park's 9km seawall (p50) trail is Vancouver's favorite outdoor hangout. Encircling the park, it offers spectacular waterfront vistas on one side and dense forest on the other. You can walk the whole thing in roughly three hours or rent a bike to cover the route far faster. Keep in mind: cyclists and in-line skaters must travel counterclockwise on the seawall, so there's no going back once you start your trundle (unless you walk).

The seawall delivers you to some of the park's top highlights. About 1.5km from the W Georgia St entrance, you'll come to the ever-popular **totem poles**, which stand tall in honor of the area's original inhabitants. The brightly painted poles were joined by some exquisitely carved Coast Salish welcome arches more recently. For the full Indigenous story, consider a fascinating **guided park walk** with Talaysay Tours (p22).

The Hollow Tree

In its early tourist destination days, a **giant western red cedar** was the park's top attraction. The tree's bottom section had a massive hollowed-out area where visitors would pose for photos, sometimes in their cars. The fragile structure still remains, and artist Douglas Coupland has celebrated it with a latter-day golden replica near the city's Marine Drive Canada Line station.

Natural Attractions

Stanley Park is studded with appeal for wildlife fans. Start at the **Lost Lagoon**, a beloved nature sanctuary near the W Georgia St entrance. On its perimeter pathway, keep your eyes peeled for blue herons and a wandering raccoon or two. Plunging deeper into the park's more secluded trails, you'll also likely spot

★ Top Tips

- It takes around three hours to walk the 9km Stanley Park seawall; bike rentals are also available on nearby Denman St.
- In summer, the seawall is packed; arrive early morning or early evening instead.
- Sidestep the Vancouver Aquarium's summer queues by making it your first stop of the day.
- Gather together a great picnic and snag a grassy spot near Lumberman's Arch.

✗ Take a Break

The handsomely renovated Prospect Point Cafe (p42) is a great spot for patio feasting in the summer; through the trees you'll see the Lions Gate Bridge.

Multitudinous dining options abound on nearby Denman St and Robson St; consider slow-cooked salmon at Forage (p53).

wrens, hummingbirds, and chittering Douglas squirrels. And while they mostly give humans a wide berth, you might also come across a coyote or two; treat them with respect and give them a wide berth as well.

For an introduction to the area's flora and fauna, start at the Stanley Park Nature House (p51). You'll find friendly volunteers and exhibits on wildlife, history and ecology – ask about its well-priced guided walks.

Beaches & Views

If it's sandy beaches you're after, the park has several alluring options. **Second Beach** is a family-friendly area on the park's western side with a grassy playground, an ice-cream-serving concession and a huge outdoor swimming **pool**. It's also close to **Ceperley Meadows**, where popular free outdoor movie screenings are staged in summer. But for a little more tranquility, try **Third Beach**. A sandy expanse with plenty of logs to sit against, this is a favored summer-evening destination for Vancouverites.

There's a plethora of additional vistas in the park, but perhaps the most popular is at **Prospect Point**. One of Vancouver's best lookouts, this lofty spot is located at the park's northern tip. In summer you'll be jostling for elbow room with tour parties; heading down the steep stairs to the viewing platform usually shakes them off. The area's recently revitalized **Prospect Point Cafe** (prospectpoint.com/dining) offers refreshments – aim for a deck table.

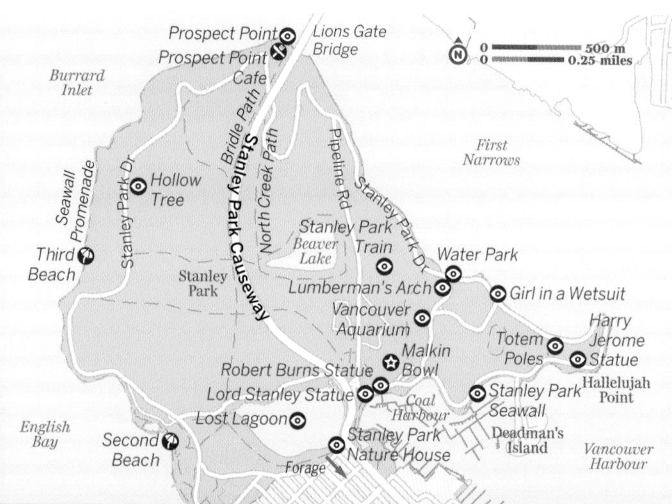

Statue Spotting

Stanley Park is studded with statues. On your leisurely amble around the tree-lined slice of heaven, you can make a game of looking out for the following.

If you're on the seawall, it shouldn't be hard to spot *Girl in a Wetsuit,* a 1972 bronze by Elek Imredy that sits in the water. But how about the **Robert Burns statue** unveiled by British prime minister Ramsay MacDonald in 1928 or the dramatic bronze of Canadian sprint legend **Harry Jerome**, who held six world records and won a bronze at the 1964 Summer Olympics.

Here's a clue for the next one: it's near Malkin Bowl (p56). Marking the first official visit to Canada by a US president, this elegant statue is actually a memorial: after visiting in 1923, Warren Harding died a week later in San Francisco.

For Kids

It doesn't take much to plan an entire day with children here. As well as the aquarium and the Nature House, there are some additional must-dos for under-10s.

Make a beeline to the waterfront **water park** near **Lumberman's Arch**, where you'll also find a playground.

Dry the kids off with a trundle on the **Stanley Park Train**. Near the aquarium (p52), this replica of the first passenger train that rolled into Vancouver in 1887 is a family favorite.

Before leaving the park, visit the man behind the fun day you've just had. Take the ramp running parallel with the seawall near the W Georgia St entrance and you'll find an almost-hidden **statue of Lord Stanley** with his arms outstretched, nestled in the trees.

On his plinth are the words he used at the park's 1889 dedication ceremony: 'To the use and enjoyment of people of all colours, creeds and customs for all time.' It's a sentiment that still resonates loudly here today.

The Poet of Stanley Park

The only person to be legally buried in Stanley Park is writer Pauline Johnson. A champion of Indigenous culture, she wrote a bestselling book on Coast Salish legends.

When she died in 1913, thousands of locals lined the streets to mark her passing. Her memorial is a few steps from the seawall's Siwash Rock landmark.

Top Experience

Peruse Paintings at the Vancouver Art Gallery

MAP P49, G3

vanartgallery.bc.ca

Residing in a heritage courthouse building but inching toward opening a fancy new venue any year now, the Vancouver Art Gallery is the region's most important art gallery. It's also a vital part of the city's cultural scene. Contemporary exhibitions – often showcasing the Vancouver School of renowned photoconceptualists – are combined with global blockbuster traveling shows.

Gallery 101

Before you arrive, check online for details of the latest exhibitions; the biggest shows of the year are typically in summer. But the gallery isn't just about blockbusters. If you have time, explore this landmark building's other offerings. Start on the top floor, where British Columbia's most famous painter is often showcased. Emily Carr (1871–1945) is celebrated for her swirling, nature-inspired paintings of regional landscapes and Indigenous culture. Watercolors were her main approach, and the gallery has a large collection of her works.

Join the Locals

The gallery isn't just a place to geek out over cool art. In fact, locals treat it as an important part of their social calendar. Every few months, the venue stages its regular **FUSE** socials, which transform the domed heritage building into a highly popular evening event with DJs, bars, live performances and quirky gallery tours. Vancouverites dress up and treat the event as one of the highlights of the city's art scene; expect a clubby vibe to pervade proceedings.

Offsite

Three blocks from the gallery on W Georgia St – in the shadow of the monolithic Shangri-La Hotel – **Offsite** is the gallery's small, somewhat incongruous, but always thought-provoking outdoor installation space. The alfresco contemporary works here are changed twice yearly and they routinely inspire passersby to whip out their camera phones for an impromptu snap or two. The installations have varied widely over the years but have included gigantic photo portraits of Chinese children and scale models of local cannery buildings.

★ Top Tips

- On Tuesdays between 5pm and 9pm, entry is by donation.
- Seniors can also partake of the by-donation entry on the first Monday of every month between 10am and 1pm.
- Check the gallery's online calendar for curator talks and expert lectures; online registration is typically recommended.

Take a Break

The large patio of the on-site **1931 Gallery Bistro** (1931gallerybistro.com) is a great spot to grab a coffee and people-watch over bustling Robson St.

For a fancy dinner to end your day out, chic Hawksworth (p54) is just a few steps away.

Walking Tour

Downtown Grand Tour

The heart of city-center Vancouver is a grid of major streets lined with shops and restaurants. But it's also home to galleries, historic buildings and an accessible rooftop garden that overlooks downtown's shimmering glass towers. Follow the route below and take your time; you'll find plenty of pit-stop cafes and coffeeshops en route.

Walk Facts

Start Olympic Cauldron

End Marine Building

Length 3km; one hour

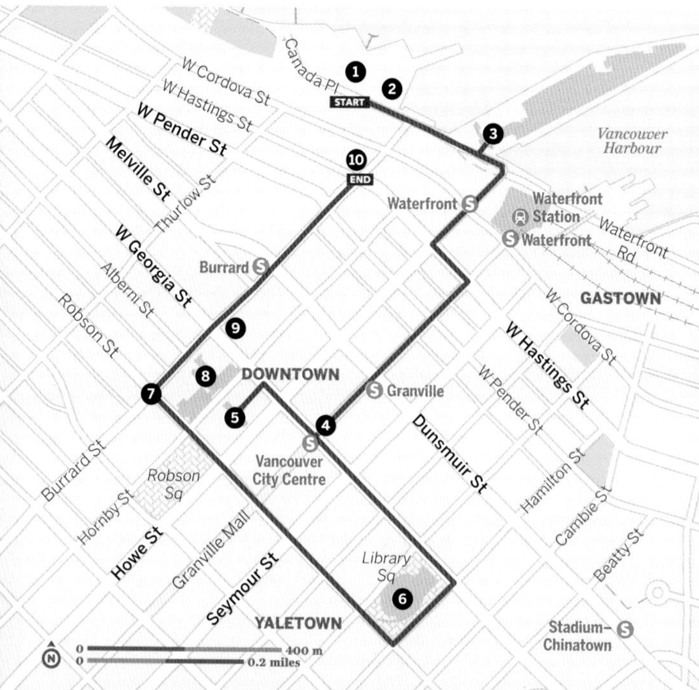

❶ Olympic Cauldron

A landmark reminder of Vancouver's 2010 Winter Olympics, check out the tripod-like Olympic Cauldron. Only occasionally lit these days, it's a great spot for photos, with a grand mountain backdrop.

❷ Convention Centre

The adjacent Convention Centre West Building hugs the waterfront. Follow its external walkway for some giant public artworks, including a pixelated orca and a bright-blue raindrop.

❸ Canada Place

The area's original convention-center building, sail-shaped Canada Place (p51) is next door. Stroll its pier-like outer promenade and watch the floatplanes taking off and landing on the water.

❹ Granville & Georgia Streets

Swap the scenic waterfront for downtown's bustling thoroughfares. You'll pass shops and cafes before reaching the ever-busy intersection of Granville and Georgia Sts.

❺ Vancouver Art Gallery

Inside a stately heritage building, the Vancouver Art Gallery (p44) is a must-do (especially the top-floor Emily Carr paintings). Ravenously hungry? Dive into the nearby food trucks for an alfresco lunch.

❻ Vancouver Public Library

There's much more than books to check out at the Colosseum-like Vancouver Public Library (p52). Press floor nine in the elevator to reach a large public garden with cityscape views.

❼ Robson & Burrard Streets

Consider your dinner options around the intersection of Robson and Burrard Sts. You'll find a tempting menu of possibilities, from spicy Thai to pub grub.

❽ Fairmont Hotel

Nip into the lobby of the city's grand-dame heritage sleepover, Fairmont Hotel Vancouver. Look for 1930s design features and the two friendly dogs that call the concierge desk home.

❾ Christ Church Cathedral

Historic Christ Church Cathedral (p52) seems incongruous among the glass towers. Gaze at its stained-glass windows and eye-popping hammerbeam ceiling.

❿ Marine Building

The spectacular Marine Building (p50) was completed during the height of the art-deco era. Give yourself plenty of time to peruse its exterior transport and maritime-themed decorative flourishes, then duck inside and gawk at its palatial lobby.

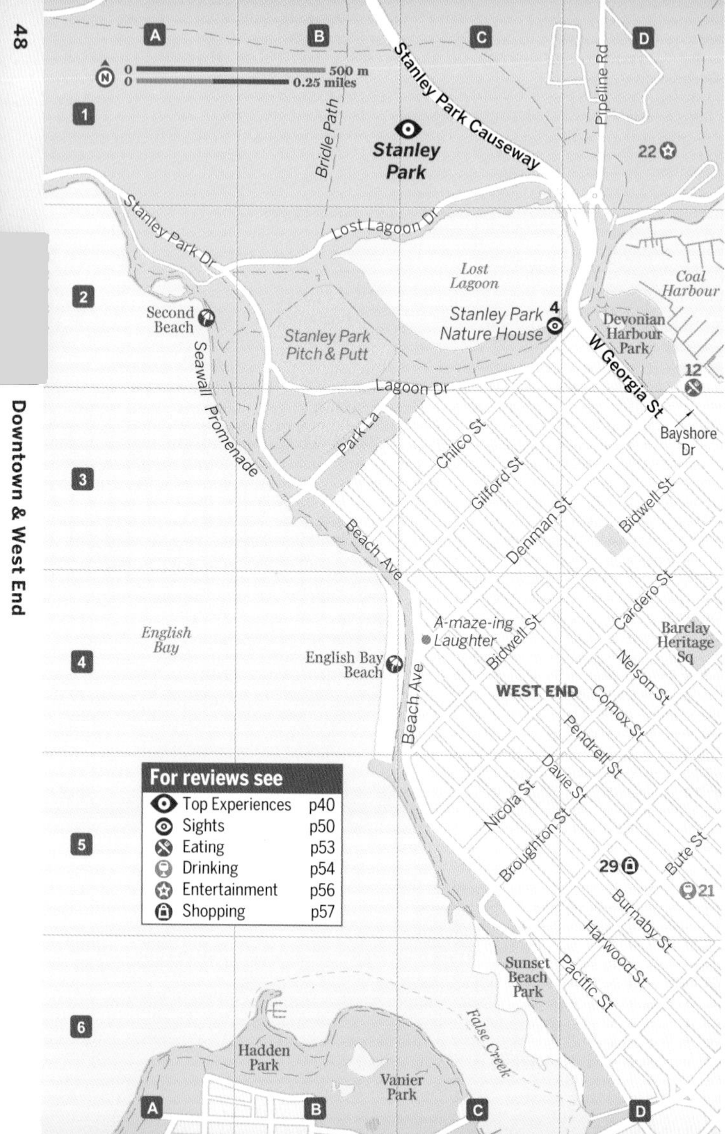
A
B
C
D
1
2
3
4
5
6
0 500 m
0 0.25 miles
Stanley Park
Stanley Park Causeway
Pipeline Rd
Bridle Path
22
Stanley Park Dr
Lost Lagoon Dr
Lost Lagoon
Coal Harbour
Second Beach
Stanley Park Nature House
4
Devonian Harbour Park
Stanley Park Pitch & Putt
Seawall Promenade
W Georgia St
12
Lagoon Dr
Park La
Chilco St
Bayshore Dr
Gilford St
Denman St
Bidwell St
Beach Ave
Cardero St
A-maze-ing Laughter
Barclay Heritage Sq
English Bay
English Bay Beach
Bidwell St
Nelson St
WEST END
Comox St
Beach Ave
Pendrell St
Davie St
For reviews see
Top Experiences p40
Sights p50
Eating p53
Drinking p54
Entertainment p56
Shopping p57
Nicola St
Broughton St
29
Bute St
21
Burnaby St
Harwood St
Sunset Beach Park
Pacific St
False Creek
Hadden Park
Vanier Park

E F G H
1 2 3 4 5 6

8 Vancouver Aquarium
Brockton Oval
Seawall Promenade
Brockton Point
Stanley Park Dr
2 Stanley Park Seawall
Hallelujah Point
Deadman's Island
HMCS Discovery Naval Training Station
17
Royal Vancouver Yacht Club
Vancouver Harbour

0 100 m
Burrard St
Bill Reid Gallery of Northwest Coast Art
7 Christ Church Cathedral
1
9 Cycle City Tours
W Georgia St
Howe St
16
Hornby St
Vancouver Art Gallery

Coal Harbour Seawall
Coal Harbour Park
Harbour Green Park
Tourism Vancouver Visitor Center
5 Canada Place
Canada Pl
Nicola St
Broughton St
W Pender St
W Cordova St
W Hastings St
18
Marine Building 3
30
Waterfront
Waterfront Rd
Waterfront Station
Jervis St
13
Melville St
W Georgia St
Alberni St
Vancouver Bullion & Currency Exchange
Burrard
See Enlargement
DOWNTOWN
Bute St
Robson St
Haro St
Barclay St
W Cordova St
W Hastings St
Granville
10
Nelson Park
Thurlow St
26
28
Vancouver City Centre
Dunsmuir St
W Pender St
Robson Sq
SkyTrain Canada Line
Vancouver Public Library
Burrard St
Hornby St
27
24
11
Richards St
Hamilton St
14
SkyTrain
20
Howe St
Helmcken St
Homer St
6
Cambie St
Stadium–Chinatown
23
Seymour St
19
Smithe St
Robson St
25
Davie St
Granville St
Nelson St
Beatty St
Griffiths Way
Drake St
YALETOWN
Mainland St
BC Place Stadium
15

Sights

Bill Reid Gallery of Northwest Coast Art GALLERY

1 MAP P49, G2

Hailed Haida artist Bill Reid (1920–98) was known for building bridges between Indigenous and settler people through his work as an artist, broadcaster and community activist.

The gallery was named in his honor, and showcases some of his artwork, as well as contemporary works by other Indigenous artists. Look for the full-scale totem pole carved by James Hart of Haida Gwaii, and a bronze masterpiece called *Mythic Messengers*, created by Reid himself. (billreidgallery.ca)

Stanley Park Seawall WATERFRONT

2 MAP P49, E2

Built between 1917 and 1980, the 9km seawall trail is Vancouver's favorite outdoor hangout. Encircling the whole of Stanley Park, it offers spectacular waterfront, mountain-fringed vistas on one side and dense forest canopy on the other.

You can walk it in around three blister-triggering hours, or rent a bike from the Denman St operators near the park entrance to cover the route faster. But what's the rush? Slow down and slide into the natural side of life instead.

Marine Building HISTORIC BUILDING

3 MAP P49, G4

Vancouver's most romantic old-school tower block, and also its

Siwash Rock, Stanley Park Seawall

BRESTER IRINA/SHUTTERSTOCK ©

best art-deco building, the elegant 22-story Marine Building is a tribute to the city's maritime past. Check out its elaborate exterior of seahorses, lobsters and streamlined steamships, then nip into the lobby, which is like a walk-through artwork. Stained-glass panels and a polished floor inlaid with signs of the zodiac await.

Stanley Park Nature House

NATURE RESERVE

4 MAP P48, C2

Illuminating the breathtaking array of flora and fauna just steps from the busy streets of the West End, this charming nature center at the north end of Alberni St is a great introduction to Stanley Park's wild side. Volunteers will tell you all you need to know about local wildlife, from coyotes to Douglas squirrels, blue herons and black-capped chickadees. Guided nature walks are also offered, or you can wander the park's trails on your own, armed with your newfound expertise. (stanleyparkecology.ca)

Canada Place

LANDMARK

5 MAP P49, H4

Vancouver's version of the Sydney Opera House – judging by the number of postcards it appears on – this iconic landmark is shaped like sails jutting into the sky over the harbor.

Both a cruise-ship terminal and a convention center, it's also a stroll-worthy pier, providing photogenic views of the busy floatplane action and looming North Shore mountains. Here for Canada Day on July 1? This is the center of the city's festivities, with displays, live music and fireworks. (canadaplace.ca;)

Stanley Park Tips

Go early Just after dawn is the best time to visit. Early-morning joggers smile as they pass by, the birds welcome you with song, and the trees tower majestically overhead.

Get lost Some of the best surprises – faces carved in tree trunks, owls perched silently above, the perfect alcove for intrigue and romance amid the ferns and firs – are only accessed by tiny paths that branch off from the main trails.

Stick to the sea A seawall stroll cements Vancouver's reputation as one of the world's most beautiful cities. Siwash Rock standing sentry over Burrard Inlet, sprawling Third Beach and downtown's glass towers stud the circuit with unforgettable vistas.

Recommended by Ernest White II, *Executive Producer & Presenter,* Fly Brother with Ernest White II. *@FlyBrother*

Vancouver Public Library

LIBRARY

6 MAP P49, G6

This dramatic Colosseum-like building must be a temple to the great god of libraries. If not, it's certainly one of the world's most magnificent book-lending facilities. Designed by Moshe Safdie and opened in 1995, its collections (including lendable musical instruments) are arranged over several floors. Head up to floor nine for the **Rooftop Garden**, a lofty, tree-lined outdoor plaza lined with tables and chairs: it's perfect for a view-hugging coffee break. (vpl.ca;)

Christ Church Cathedral

CATHEDRAL

7 MAP P49, G2

Completed in 1895 and designated a cathedral in 1929, the city's most attractive Gothic-style church is nestled incongruously alongside looming glass towers.

When services aren't being held, casual visitors are warmly welcomed: check out the dramatic hammerbeam wooden ceiling plus the slender glass-encased bell tower that was recently added to the exterior. The cathedral is also home to a wide range of cultural events, including regular choir and chamber-music recitals and the occasional Shakespeare reading. (thecathedral.ca)

Vancouver Aquarium

AQUARIUM

8 MAP P49, E1

Canada's largest aquarium and Stanley Park's biggest draw, Vancouver Aquarium is home to more than 65,000 animals. It's also a center for marine research, ocean literacy and climate activism.

The sea otters have unofficial celebrity status in the city, and the sea lions (one weighing in at 862kg) are show-stoppers.

Animal-welfare groups say keeping cetaceans in enclosed tanks is harmful for these complex animals, and the Vancouver Park Board has made legal moves in recent years to ban the aquarium from keeping them. (vanaqua.org)

Urban Birding

Birding has become a popular pastime for many Vancouverites and if you're keen to join in the fun, head to Stanley Park (p40), **Vanier Park**, **Pacific Spirit Park** or Queen Elizabeth Park (p120). Many city streets are also home to a diverse array of beak-tastic critters: on a West End exploration, you may spot hummingbirds, barred owls and northern flicker woodpeckers. Heading into adjoining Stanley Park, you might also see bald eagles, cormorants and herons – which are famous for nesting in a large and noisy heronry here every spring.

Cycle City Tours

CYCLING

9 MAP P49, H2

Striped with bike lanes, Vancouver is a good city for two-wheeled exploring. But if you're not great at navigating, consider a guided tour with this popular operator. Its Grand Tour ($90) is a great city intro, while the Craft Beer Tour ($90) includes brunch and three breweries. Alternatively, go solo with a rental; there's a bike lane outside the store. (cyclevancouver.com)

Eating

Boulevard Kitchen & Oyster Bar

SEAFOOD $$$

10 MAP P49, F5

Award-winning executive chefs Alex Chen and Roger Ma are the masterminds behind the sophisticated seafood-forward menu here. Precision and presentation impress, as do the flavor combinations.

Start with a seafood tower, a feast for the eyes and the belly: the multilayered masterpiece includes nori-wrapped steelhead, albacore-tuna tataki and (of course) oysters. Find Boulevard Kitchen within the Sutton Place Hotel Vancouver. (boulevardvancouver.ca)

Japadog

JAPANESE $

11 MAP P49, G6

You'll have spotted the lunchtime queues at the Japadog hot-dog stands around town, but this was the first storefront, opening back in 2010. The ever-*genki* Japanese expats serve up a menu of lip-smacking wonder wieners – the likes of turkey smokies with miso sauce and crunchy shrimp tempura dogs – but there are also irresistible fries (try the butter and *shoyu* version). (japadog.com)

Local Dining

Restaurants on Robson St are always lined with tourists, but locals are much more likely to be dining out at the better-priced neighborhood eateries on Denman and Davie Sts in the West End, including Japanese, Spanish and Indian options.

Yasma

CAFE $

12 MAP P48, D2

Located right on the waterfront in Vancouver's stunning seaside Coal Harbour neighborhood, Yasma serves up celebrated cuisines from Syria and Lebanon.

You'll find modern takes on Middle Eastern staples here, ranging from flavorful dips made from scratch (the Muhammara dip is a must-try) to lamb dishes to regional specialties found nowhere else in the city. (yasma.ca)

Forage

CANADIAN $$

A popular farm-to-table eatery, this sustainability-focused restaurant is the perfect way to sample regional flavors. Brunch has become a firm local favorite (halibut eggs Benny recommended), and for dinner there's everything from bison steaks to slow-cooked salmon. Add a flight of BC craft beers, with top choices from the likes of Four Winds, Strange Fellows and more. Reservations are recommended. (foragevancouver.com)

Jam Cafe

BREAKFAST $

14 MAP P49, H5

The Vancouver outpost of Victoria's wildly popular breakfast and brunch superstar draws the city's longest queues, especially on weekends. Reservations are not accepted, so you're advised to dine off-peak and during the week. You'll find a white-walled room studded with Canadian knickknacks and a huge array of satisfying options, from chicken and biscuits to red-velvet pancakes. (jamcafes.com)

Chief of the Undersea World, Vancouver Aquarium (p52)

SOUTH FJORD MEDIA/SHUTTERSTOCK ©; ARTIST: BILL REID ©

Tacofino

MEXICAN $$

15 MAP P49, F6

Fresh West Coast flavors meet Mexican food staples at this street-food-style place. It started as a small food truck in Tofino, BC's surf town, and has quickly become a go-to food joint with seven locations scattered around the city. Pacific cod tacos and crunchy carnitas beckon taco-loving crowds, day and night. (tacofino.com)

Hawksworth

NORTHWESTERN US $$$

16 MAP P49, H3

The fine-dining anchor of the top-end Rosewood Hotel Georgia is a see-and-be-seen spot for swank dates and business meetings. Created by and named after one of Vancouver's top chefs, its menu fuses contemporary West Coast approaches with clever international influences, hence dishes such as ling cod with orange lassi. There is also a *prix fixe* lunch ($28). (hawksworthrestaurant.com)

Drinking

Lift Bar & Grill

BAR

17 MAP P49, E2

On warmer days, grab bevvies on this bustling rooftop bar and take in scenic Stanley Park views while enjoying a summer sipper. In the mood for a cocktail? Try a rosemary fizz (on the rocks), a bourbon sour or a blood-orange bellini. Or go for a pint of on-tap local beer. Happy hour is 3pm to 5:30pm daily. (liftbarandgrill.com)

Botanist COCKTAIL BAR

18 MAP P49, G4

Hands down Vancouver's top cocktail bar (as its endless list of accolades will attest), Botanist combines chemist-like cocktail designs with amazing artistry to create magic in a glass. Head bartender Jeff Savage serves up the likes of 'what the flower,' combining electric daisies with gin and cherry-blossom tea. Each drink comes complete with a whimsical tale, too. (botanistrestaurant.com)

Uva Wine & Cocktail Bar LOUNGE

19 MAP P49, F6

This sexy nook fuses a heritage mosaic floor with a dash of mod class. Despite the cool appearances, there's a snob-free approach that encourages taste-tripping through an extensive by-the-glass wine menu and some dangerously delicious cocktails – we love the diplomat. Food is part of the mix (including shareable small plates) and there's a daily 2pm to 5pm happy hour. (uvavancouver.com)

Fountainhead Pub GAY

20 MAP P49, E6

The area's loudest and proudest gay neighborhood pub, this friendly joint is all about the patio, whose denizens spill onto Davie St like the contents of an overturned wine glass. Join the summer-evening pastime of watching passersby or retreat to a quieter spot inside for a few lagers or a naughty cocktail: anyone for a crispy crotch or a slippery nipple? (fthdpub.com)

Citizen of the Century

Born in Trinidad in 1863, **Joe Fortes** arrived in Vancouver in 1885, when only a few hundred African American men lived in the fledgling townsite. Reputedly saving a mother and child during the area's 1886 **Great Fire**, he later settled around English Bay in the West End. From here, he became a self-appointed lifeguard, saving dozens of lives and teaching thousands of children to swim over the years.

The city made him its first official lifeguard in 1897, presenting him with a gold watch for devoted service in 1910. When he died in 1922, his funeral was one of the biggest in Vancouver. Fortes' memory lives on: a city restaurant and a public library are named after him, Canada Post released a stamp depicting him in 2013, and the Vancouver Historical Society named him 'Citizen of the Century' in 1986.

1181 GAY

21 MAP P48, D5

A change of ownership is revitalizing this intimate Davie St 'gayborhood' mainstay, a loungey, two-room late-night hangout where flirty cocktails rule. Check ahead for events, but expect a wide array of options from drag nights to improv comedy to DJ dance parties. This is the area's classiest gay bar. (facebook.com/1181Lounge)

Entertainment

Theatre Under the Stars PERFORMING ARTS

22 MAP P48, D1

The charming **Malkin Bowl** (malkinbowl.com) provides an atmospheric alfresco stage for the summertime TUTS season, usually featuring two interchanging Broadway musicals. It's hard to find a better place to catch a show, especially as the sun fades over the surrounding Stanley Park (p40) trees. The troupe's production values have massively increased in recent years, and these productions are slick, professional and energetic. (tuts.ca)

Cinematheque CINEMA

23 MAP P49, E6

This beloved cinema operates like an ongoing film festival with a daily-changing program of movies. A $3 annual membership is required – organize it at the door – before you can skulk in the dark with other movie buffs who probably named their children (or pets) after Fellini and Bergman. (thecinematheque.ca)

Commodore Ballroom LIVE MUSIC

24 MAP P49, F6

Local bands know they've made it when they play Vancouver's best midsized venue, a restored art-deco ballroom that has the city's bounciest dance floor – courtesy of tires being placed under its floorboards. If you need a break from moshing, collapse at a table lining the perimeter, catch your breath with a bottled brew and then plunge back in. (commodoreballroom.com)

Vancouver Canucks HOCKEY

25  MAP P49, H6

Recent years haven't been hugely successful for Vancouver's

Vancouver's Favorite Public Artwork

Head toward the West End's English Bay Beach and you'll be stopped in your tracks by 14 very tall men. **A-maze-ing Laughter** by Yue Minjun comprises a gathering of oversized bronze figures permanently engaged in a hearty round of chuckling. It's a permanent artwork legacy from the city's **Vancouver Biennale** (vancouverbiennale.com); check its website for additional artsy installations.

National Hockey League (NHL) team, which means it's sometimes easy to snag tickets to a game if you're simply visiting and want to see what 'ice hockey' (no one calls it that here) is all about. You'll hear 'go Canucks, go!' booming from the seats and in local bars on game nights. (nhl.com/canucks)

Shopping

Paper Hound

BOOKS

26 MAP P49, H5

Proving the printed word is alive and kicking, this small but perfectly curated secondhand bookstore is a dog-eared favorite among locals. A perfect spot for browsing, it has tempting tomes (mostly used but some new) on everything from nature to poetry to chaos theory. Ask for recommendations; they really know their stuff here. Don't miss the bargain rack out front. (paperhound.ca)

Golden Age Collectables

BOOKS

27 MAP P49, F5

If you're missing your regular dose of *Hulkverines* or you just want to blow your vacation budget on a highly detailed life-size model of Conan the Barbarian, head straight to this Aladdin's cave of the comic-book world. The staff is friendly and welcoming – especially to wide-eyed kids buying their first *Amazing Spider-Man*. (gacvan.com)

Hunter & Hare

VINTAGE

28 MAP P49, H5

A lovely little store specializing in well-curated consignment clothing and accessories for women, this is the place to head to if you've left your summer frock at home. Staff can point you in the right direction and prices are enticingly reasonable. It's not all used togs; there's also jewelry, greeting cards and beauty products from local artisan producers. (hunterandhare.com)

Little Sister's Book & Art Emporium

BOOKS

29 MAP P48, D5

Launched almost 40 years ago as one of the only LGBTIQ+ bookstores in Canada, Little Sister's is a bazaar of queer-positive tomes, plus magazines, clothing and toys of the adult type. If this is your first visit to Vancouver, it's a great place to network with the local 'gayborhood.' Check the noticeboards for events and announcements from the community. (littlesisters.ca)

Mink Chocolates

FOOD

30 MAP P49, G4

If chocolate is the main food group in your book, follow your candy-primed nose to this choccy shop and cafe in the downtown core. Select from the array of colorfully boxed ganache-filled bars, including top-seller Mermaid's Choice, then hit the drinks bar for the best velvety hot choc you've ever tasted. (minkchocolates.com)

Walking Tour

Lower Lonsdale Wander

This loop through Lower Lonsdale will take you into the heart of North Vancouver's reinvented Shipyards District. You'll discover a once-gritty industrial zone that's been reinvigorated with oceanfront attractions, scenic boardwalk promenades and a full menu of tasty pit stops. Take your time here; there's lots to discover.

Walk Facts

Start Lonsdale Quay SeaBus Station

End Burgoo Bistro

Length 1km; one hour

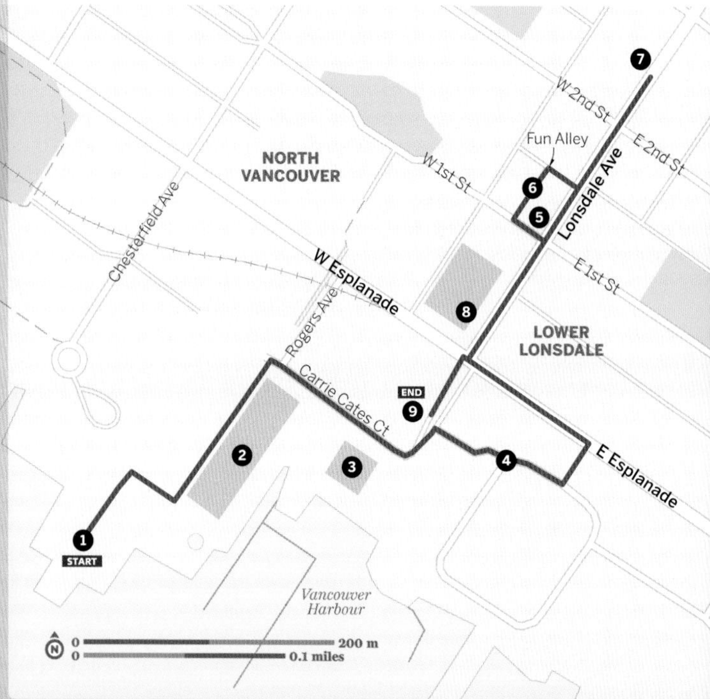

❶ Lonsdale Quay

After your 15-minute SeaBus voyage from Vancouver's Waterfront Station, walk up the ramp at North Van's Lonsdale Quay and turn right.

❷ Lonsdale Quay Market

The **Lonsdale Quay Market** (lonsdalequay.com) is lined with food stands and artisan stores; there's even an on-site microbrewery if you're thirsty.

❸ Polygon Gallery

A symbol of the area's revitalization, visit the striking **Polygon Gallery** (thepolygon.ca). And check out the upper-floor views across to downtown Vancouver.

❹ Old Wallace Shipyards

Look for the large-format photo of the yesteryear shipyard, showing hundreds of tough-as-nails men gearing up for work.

❺ Lift Breakfast Bakery

Revive yourself with coffee and treats at **Lift** (liftonlonsdale.ca), serving breakfast, brunch and weekend dinner.

❻ Fun Alley

Right next door, a tiny back alley has been painted like a walk-through kaleidoscope via, a mural project by young local artists.

❼ Hunter & Hare

Located further north at 225 Lonsdale Ave, this classy women's consignment store offers a stylish selection of name-brand fashion finds at reasonable prices, as well as a selection of new jewelry pieces, accessories and home goods. This bright, modern space is the perfect spot to pick up that perfect pair of jeans and a cute keepsake for your friend, too.

❽ Mo's General Store

Quirky souvenir shopping is easy at **Mo's General Store** (mosgeneralstore.com). Where else would you find woolen avocado socks?

❾ Burgoo

Conclude your day out with dinner at this popular bistro-style **restaurant** (burgoo.ca). The SeaBus terminal, and a short hop back to downtown Vancouver, are just steps away.

Top Experience

Teeter Above the Treetops at Capilano Suspension Bridge Park

Wobbling along the Capilano Suspension Bridge, suspended 70m high above the Capilano River, has been an epic experience enjoyed by visitors since the bridge was built in 1883. On the other side, Treetops Adventure offers a series of seven small suspension bridges connecting trekkers to viewing platforms that perch above old-growth Douglas firs, some as much as 1300 years old.

capbridge.com

Bridge

Starting life as a simple rope-and-plank span in 1880, the bridge's current steel-cable iteration stretches 137m; wide enough to fly two Boeing 747s wing-to-wing underneath (strangely, no one has tried this yet). You'll sway gently as you walk across (unless a group of deliberately heavy-footed teenagers is stomping nearby): most first-timers steady themselves on the cable 'handrail' but usually let go as they progress and adapt to the leg-wobbling sensation. Don't forget to stop midway for photos of the mountain-framed, tree-lined vista.

Park

The bridge is the star attraction, but there's much more to keep you occupied here. Check the outdoor historic displays and Indigenous totem poles before you head across the bridge. On the other side, walk above a rainforest canopy at **Treetops Adventure**, shimmy along the adrenaline-pumping **Cliffwalk** – a cantilevered walkway – or if you'd prefer to explore with your feet planted firmly on the ground, wooden boardwalks weave along the forest floor.

Birds of Prey

Get up close with a great horned owl or stand within arm's reach of a bald eagle at the **Birds of Raptors Ridge**, an on-site educational facility committed to educating the public on birds of prey such as owls, raptors and falcons. It's open every weekend in April and May, and every day between June and September.

★ Top Tips

- Arrive soon after opening time to avoid the relentless summer crush.
- Take the free year-round shuttle bus from downtown Vancouver to the park's entrance.
- The gift shop is one of Metro Vancouver's biggest; you can tick off your entire souvenir list in one go here.
- Free shuttle bus from downtown or transit bus 236 from Lonsdale Quay.
- Grouse Mountain (p17) is 10 minutes north on the same 236 transit bus route.

Take a Break

The park's bistro-like **Cliff House Restaurant** (capbridge.com) serves great fish and chips plus local craft beer; peruse the yesteryear Capilano photos on the walls.

Explore

Gastown & Chinatown

As the city's oldest downtown neighborhood, Gastown combines cobblestone streets and heritage buildings with modern galleries and trendy bars. The historic 12-block stretch is a hub for shopping and entertainment. Next door is one of Canada's largest Chinatown districts, a vibrant community dotted with dim sum restaurants, traditional bakeries and food shops, and hip, hidden cocktail spots.

The Short List

- ***Alibi Room (p74)*** *Tucking into the city's best array of regional craft beers while rubbing shoulders with the locals at one of the long, candlelit tables; small sampler glasses recommended.*
- ***Eastside Flea (p76)*** *Nosing around the artisan stalls, vintage-clothing stands and tasty food trucks at this regular hipster market.*
- ***St Lawrence Restaurant (p73)*** *Feasting on fine French Canadian cuisine and feeling like you're hanging out in old-town Montréal.*

Getting There & Around

SkyTrain's Waterfront Station is at the western edge of Gastown. Stadium-Chinatown Station is at the edge of Chinatown, due south of Gastown.

Bus 14 heads northwards from downtown's Granville St, then along Hastings, handy for both Gastown and Chinatown. Buses 3, 4, 7 and 8 also service the area.

There's metered parking throughout Gastown and Chinatown.

Gastown & Chinatown Map on p68

Maple Tree Sq (p72), Gastown ALENA CHARYKOVA/SHUTTERSTOCK ©

Top Experience

Sip Tea at Dr Sun Yat-Sen Classical Chinese Garden

Reputedly the first Chinese 'scholars' garden' ever built outside China, and opened just in time for Vancouver's Expo '86 world exposition, this oasis of tranquility with its covered walkways is one of the city's most beloved ornamental green spaces. Framed by tile-topped walls and centered on a mirror-calm pond fringed with twisting trees, the garden offers respite from clamorous Chinatown.

MAP P68, D4

vancouverchinesegarden.com

Harmonious Design

With symbol-heavy architecture that feels centuries old – walled courtyards, small bridges, flared-roof buildings, and sidewalks fashioned from mosaics of patterned pebbles – this highly photogenic garden is also studded with large, eerie **limestone rocks** that look as though they were imported from the moon. In reality, they were hauled all the way from Lake Tai in China. They give the garden a mystical, almost otherworldly feel.

Natural Jewels

The garden's large, lily-pad-covered **pond** is often as calm as a sheet of green glass – except when its resident neon-orange koi carp break the surface in hopes of snagging food from passersby (don't feed them, though). They're not the only critters that call this watery haven home. Look carefully at some of the rocks poking from the water and you'll spot dozing turtles basking in the sun. Ducks, frogs and beady-eyed herons are also frequently seen. Plant-wise, you'll find pine, bamboo, flowering plum trees and pots of decades-old bonsai trees that look like the diminutive offspring of Tolkien's Ents.

Freebie Alternative

Located right next door to the paid-entry garden, a fancy-free gratis alternative shares some of its sibling's classical features. The **Dr Sun Yat-Sen Park** was inspired by the adjoining attraction and shares the same pond. It also has nature-fringed walkways encircled by tile-topped walls, and its main feature is a small, red-roofed, Chinese-style pavilion that makes for great photos, especially when you catch it reflected off the pond.

★ Top Tips

- Arrive early in summer to experience the tranquility before the crowds roll in.
- Tours run hourly during the summer peak, and several times a day the rest of the year. Check the schedule online.
- Peruse the gift shop before you leave; it's well stocked with tea and traditional calligraphy tools.
- The towering Chinatown Millennium Gate (p69) is one block away if your camera still has some battery power.

✂ Take a Break

Tuck into a retro-style booth and lunch on family barbecue dishes at **Chinatown BBQ** (chinatownbbq.com).

For dinner, E Pender is also home to Sai Woo (p71), the perfect place for cocktails and soy-ginger chicken.

Walking Tour

Chinatown Culture & History Crawl

One of North America's largest and most historic Chinatown districts, Vancouver's Chinatown is perfect for on-foot exploration. Keep your eyes peeled for tile-topped heritage buildings, traditional grocery and apothecary stores, and street lamps adorned with fierce-looking golden dragons.

Walk Facts

Start Chinatown Millennium Gate

End Vancouver Police Museum

Length 1.5km; one hour

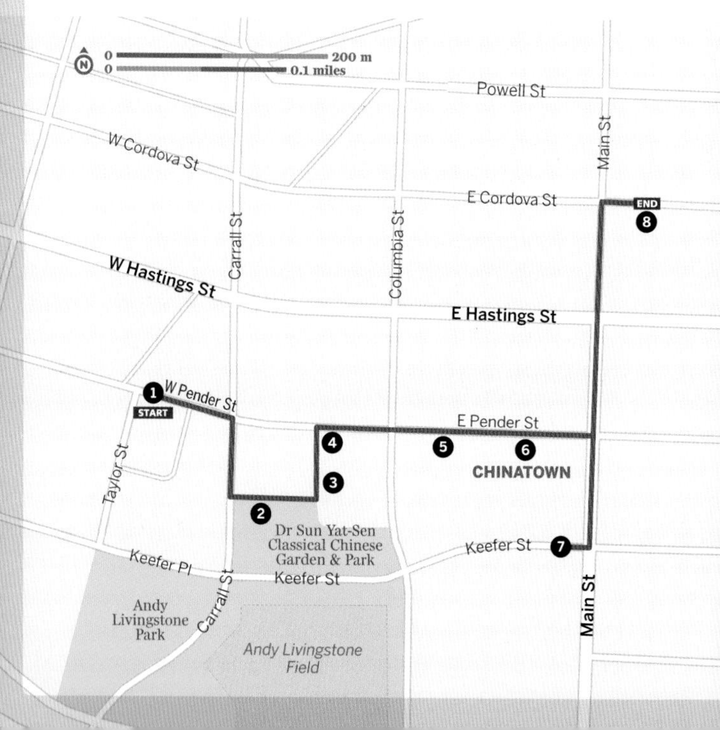

❶ Chinatown Millennium Gate

The grand entrance to Chinatown (p69) was only erected in 2000, but it's a fitting testament to the neighborhood's longevity. Crane your neck for the colorful upper-level decoration and don't miss the ground-level lion statues.

❷ Dr Sun Yat-Sen Classical Chinese Garden

Enjoy a peaceful respite from Chinatown's clamorous streets as you wander the pebble-cobbled pathways of this popular horticultural site (p64). Watch for carp and turtles in the mirror-calm pond en route.

❸ Bronze Memorial

Near the garden's entrance, wander across the small paved plaza and look for an intriguing bronze memorial set in bright-red wall tiles. It recalls the contribution of Chinese workers to the enormous project of building Canada's railway system.

❹ The 'Other' Chinatown Gate

A few steps away is a ghostly white alternative Chinatown gate. Built for Vancouver's Expo '86, this one is smaller than the Millennium Gate and was moved here after the big event.

❺ Sai Woo

If you've yet to make dinner plans, peruse your options at this popular restaurant (p71). And make sure you snap a photo of its neon rooster sign, a replica of an original that was here for decades.

❻ Chinatown Storytelling Centre

A showcase of Vancouver's Chinese Canadian history, the Storytelling Centre (p70) includes a life-size diorama, an interactive etiquette table and a living legacy project highlighting the most famous Chinese Canadians from past and present.

❼ Keefer Street Stores

Chinatown is lined with a fascinating fusion of old-fashioned and far newer storefronts. Exploring Keefer St, you'll find traditional grocery shops next to hipster coffeehouses.

❽ Vancouver Police Museum

The city's crime-addled past is on colorful display at this under-the-radar museum (p69). Don't miss its historic crime exhibits and preserved mortuary room.

For reviews see

Top Experiences	p64
Sights	p69
Eating	p70
Drinking	p74
Entertainment	p75
Shopping	p76

A B C D E F
1 2 3 4
Waterfront
Waterfront Station
Sky Train Canada Line
Vancouver Harbour
0 200 m
0 0.1 miles
Waterfront Rd
Portside Park
24
2 Steam Clock
GASTOWN
Water St
22
12
13
Alexander St
Railway St
Seymour St
W Hastings St
Trounce Al
Blood Al
9
16
11
Powell St
14
Cambie St
W Cordova St
Abbott St
Dominion Building
Flack Block
6
Dunlevy Ave
Oppenheimer Park
Gore Ave
Richards St
W Pender St
Dunsmuir St
Homer St
Victory Sq
Woodward's
Carrall St
E Cordova St
15
Sins of the City Walking Tour 3
19
5
Hamilton St
Chinatown Millennium Gate 1
E Hastings St
Columbia St
Chinatown Storytelling Centre
18
Cambie St
Beatty St
W Pender St
E Pender St
Jackson Ave
Dr Sun Yat-Sen Classical Chinese Garden & Park
Taylor St
8
4
Main St
CHINATOWN
Stadium–Chinatown
17
10
Keefer Pl
Keefer St
SkyTrain
Andy Livingstone Park
20
E Georgia St
23
7
21

Sights

Chinatown Millennium Gate

LANDMARK

1 MAP P68, C3

Inaugurated in 2002, Chinatown's towering entrance is the landmark most visitors look for. Stand well back, since the decoration is mostly on its lofty upper reaches, an elaborately painted section topped with a terra-cotta-tiled roof. The characters inscribed on its eastern front implore you to 'Remember the past and look forward to the future.'

Steam Clock

LANDMARK

2 MAP P68, B2

Halfway along Water St, this oddly popular tourist magnet lures the cameras with its tooting steam whistle. Built in 1977, the clock's mechanism is actually driven by electricity; only the pipes on top are steam fueled (reveal that to the patiently waiting tourists and you might cause a riot). It sounds every 15 minutes, and marks each hour with little whistling symphonies.

Sins of the City Walking Tour

WALKING

3 MAP P68, E3

If your criminal interests are triggered by the **Vancouver Police Museum** (vancouverpolicemuseum), take one of its excellent Sins of the City walking tours, which weave through Gastown and Chinatown in search of former brothels, opium dens, gambling houses

Steam Clock

and more. The tours last up to two hours and are a great way to see the far-less-salubrious side of the shiny, glass-towered metropolis. (sinsofthecity.ca)

Chinatown Storytelling Centre MUSEUM

4 MAP P68, D4

Immersive and interactive exhibits showcase how Vancouver's Chinese Canadian history helped shape the city's past and continues to influence the present. It's the first permanent exhibit of its kind in Canada. (chinatownstorytellingcentre.org)

Eating

Ovaltine Cafe DINER $

5 MAP P68, E3

Like being inside Edward Hopper's *Nighthawks* diner painting, this time-capsule greasy spoon instantly transports you to the 1940s. Snag a booth alongside the hospital-green walls or, better yet, slide onto a tape-repaired spinning stool at the long counter. Truck-stop coffee is de rigueur here, alongside burgers, sandwiches and fried breakfasts that haven't changed in decades (yes, that's liver and onions on the menu). (facebook.com/ovaltinecafe)

Tacofino Taco Bar MEXICAN $

6 MAP P68, C2

Food-truck favorite Tacofino made an instant splash with this huge, handsome dining room featuring stylish geometric-patterned floors, hive-like lampshades and a tiny back patio.

The simple menu focuses on a handful of taco options plus nachos, soups and beer, agave and tequila flights. Fish tacos are the top seller, but the super-tender lamb *birria* version is also a strong contender. (tacofino.com;)

Phnom Penh VIETNAMESE, CAMBODIAN $

7 MAP P68, E4

The dishes at this bustling local legend are split between

Beyond the Steam Clock

Walking along Water St, you'll likely bump into a gaggle of visitors snapping photos of the Steam Clock (p69), a freestanding timepiece famous for its time-marking steam-whistle displays. But Gastown is full of additional photo opportunities, as long as you know where to go. Scan for cool architectural details at the **Dominion Building** and the **Flack Block**, both in Hastings St, gawk at **Gaoler's Mews** with its heritage redbrick and cobblestone courtyard, and try to get the perfect angle to snap the old and new neon 'W' signs at the renovated **Woodward's Building**, also in Hastings St.

Cambodian and Vietnamese soul-food classics. It's the highly addictive chicken wings and their lovely pepper sauce that keep regulars loyal. Once you've piled up the bones, dive back in for round two: papaya salad, butter beef and spring rolls show just how good a street-food-inspired Asian menu can be. (phnompenhrestaurant.ca)

Sai Woo

ASIAN $$

8 MAP P68, D4

There's a film-set look to the exterior of this contemporary place that resembles a replica of an old Hong Kong restaurant. But the long, slender interior is a candlelit cave with a lounge-like vibe. Expect a wide array of Asian dishes, from Szechuan spicy-beef noodles to Korean-style barbecued-pork pancakes, and consider the happy hour (5pm to 6pm), with half-price dumplings. (saiwoo.ca)

MeeT in Gastown

VEGAN $

9 MAP P68, C2

Serving great vegan comfort dishes without the rabbit-food approach, this wildly popular spot can be clamorously busy at times. But it's worth the wait for a wide-ranging array of herbivore- and carnivore-pleasing choices, from rice bowls and mac 'n' cheese (made from vegan cashew 'cheese') to hearty burgers and poutine-like fries slathered in nut-based miso gravy (highly recommended). (meetonmain.com)

Foodie Favorites

Experience a tantalizing culinary journey with my picks: Torafuku, Phnom Penh, and Elisa.

Torafuku First, indulge in a fusion of Taiwanese flavors and culture at Torafuku, where East meets West in exquisite dishes and cocktails crafted with precision and creativity.

Phnom Penh Next, step into Phnom Penh, an authentic Cambodian haven, and savor the rich aromas and bold spices that bring its traditional recipes to life. Phnom Penh offers an unforgettable taste of Southeast Asia, from noodles to its famous butter beef.

Elisa Finally, visit steakhouse paradise Elisa, where prime cuts are expertly prepared and grilled to perfection. Immerse yourself in the refined elegance of its contemporary ambience and savor the exceptional flavors that will satisfy even the most discerning palates.

Recommended by Leila Kwok, *food photographer. @leilalikes*

Vancouver's Oldest Street?

Just a few weeks after it renamed itself Vancouver in 1886 (no one liked the original name 'Granville,' nor the insalubrious slang name 'Gastown' that preceded it), the fledgling city of around 1000 homes burnt almost to the ground in what came to be known as the **Great Fire**. But the locals weren't about to jump on the next boat out of town. Within days, plans were drawn up for a new city, this time favoring brick and stone over wood.

Starting Again

The first buildings to be erected radiated from Maple Tree Sq, in particular along Carrall St. This short thoroughfare still exists today, linking the historic center of Gastown to Chinatown. Take a stroll along Carrall and you'll spot some grand buildings from Vancouver's early days. Some of the sturdiest structures around, they'll likely survive for many years, whether or not there's another fire.

Saving Gastown

If you'd visited 30 years ago, however, you would have seen many of these buildings seemingly on their last legs. This part of Vancouver hadn't attracted development or investment for years, and Carrall St's old taverns, hotels and storefronts were spiraling into skid-row degradation.

Two things averted the apparently inevitable. First, historians and heritage fans banded together to draw attention to the area's role in the city's founding years, a campaign that culminated in a national-historic-site designation in 2010. Second, gentrification took hold.

Gentrify for Good

With few areas around the city still left to 'enhance,' the developers finally returned to Gastown. While gentrification has many vocal detractors, an undeniable positive is that it has preserved and protected this neighborhood's historic buildings for decades to come. Carrall St's brick-and-stone landmarks have, for the most part, been sympathetically restored and renovated, giving many of them a new lease on life.

Bao Bei

CHINESE $$

10 MAP P68, D4

Reinterpreting a Chinatown heritage building with hipsteresque flourishes, this Chinese brasserie is a seductive dinner destination. Bringing a contemporary edge to Asian cuisine are tapas-sized, MSG-free dishes such as *shao bing* (stuffed Chinese flatbread), delectable dumplings and spicy-chicken steamed buns.

There's also an enticing drinks menu guaranteed to make you linger, especially if you dive into the inventive cocktails. (bao-bei.ca)

St Lawrence Restaurant

FRENCH $$$

11 MAP P68, E2

Resembling a handsome wood-floored bistro that's been teleported straight from Montréal, this sparkling, country-chic dining room is a Railtown superstar.

The Québecois approach carries over into a small menu of elevated, perfectly prepared old-school mains such as trout in brown-butter sauce and utterly delicious duck-leg confit with sausage. This is French Canadian special-occasion dining at its finest. (stlawrencerestaurant.com)

Tacofino Taco Bar (p70)

Drinking

Guilt & Co

BAR

12 MAP P68, D2

This cavelike bar beneath Gastown's brick-cobbled sidewalks is also a brilliant venue to catch some live music. Most shows are pay-what-you-can and range from trumpet jazz to heartfelt performances by singer-songwriters.

There's a great cocktail list, plus a small array of draft beers (and many more in cans and bottles). It is best to avoid weekends, when there are often long queues. (guiltandcompany.com)

Alibi Room

PUB

13 MAP P68, E2

Vancouver's best craft-beer tavern pours a near-legendary roster of 50-plus drafts, many from celebrated BC breweries, including Four Winds, Yellow Dog and Dageraad. Hipsters and veteran-ale fans alike love the 'frat bat': choose your own four samples or ask to be surprised. Check the board for new guest casks and stick around for a gastropub dinner at one of the long communal tables. (alibi.ca)

Revolver

COFFEE

14 MAP P68, B2

Gastown's coolest see-and-be-seen coffee shop, Revolver has never lost its hipster crown. But it's remained at the top of the Vancouver coffee-mug tree via a serious commitment to serving expertly prepared, top-quality java. Aim for a little booth table or, if they're taken (they usually are), hit the large communal table next door. (revolvercoffee.ca)

Back & Forth Bar

BAR

15 MAP P68, D3

There's an inviting, den-like feel to this cool-but-friendly games-room bar, where six ping-pong tables combine perfectly with a

Vancouver's Best Art Fest

During November's **Eastside Culture Crawl** (culturecrawl.ca), hundreds of local artists open their studios, houses and workshops to art-loving visitors. Festival locations stretch eastwards from the north end of Main St and visitors spend their time walking the streets looking for the next hot spot, which is typically just around the corner. Look out for the occasional street performer keeping things lively and be sure to incorporate a coffee-shop pit stop along the way. The event is a great opportunity to buy one-of-a-kind artwork souvenirs for that difficult person back home (you know the one).

12-tap beer selection (local microbrews and 'ironic' Lucky Lager included).

It's an ideal late-night hangout; book ahead for a table (from $10 to $25 per hour, with lowest rates from Sunday to Tuesday) or just indulge in some giggle-triggering games like Jenga and Pictionary. (backandforthbar.com)

Six Acres BAR

16 MAP P68, C2

At Gastown's coziest tavern you can cover all the necessary food groups via the carefully chosen draft- and bottled-beer list. There's a small, animated summer patio out front, but inside (especially upstairs) is great for hiding in a chatty, candlelit corner and working your way through the brews – plus a shared small plate or three (check out the sausage board). (sixacres.ca)

Keefer Bar COCKTAIL BAR

17 MAP P68, D4

This dark, narrow and atmospheric Chinatown bar has been claimed by local cocktail-loving coolsters since day one. Drop in for a full evening of liquid tasting and you'll have a blast. From perfectly prepared rosemary gimlets and tart blood moons to an excellent whiskey menu and some tasty tapas (the steam buns are top-notch), it offers up a great night out. (thekeeferbar.com)

Revolver

Entertainment

Rickshaw Theatre LIVE MUSIC

18 MAP P68, E3

Revamped from its grungy 1970s incarnation, the funky Rickshaw shows that Eastside gentrification can be positive. The stage of choice for many punk and indie acts, it's an excellent place to see a band. There's a huge mosh area near the stage and rows of theater-style seats at the back. (liveatrickshaw.com)

Firehall Arts Centre THEATER

19 MAP P68, E3

One of the leading players in Vancouver's independent-theater scene, this intimate, studio-sized

Eastside Flea

venue is located inside a historic former fire station. It presents culturally diverse contemporary drama and dance, with an emphasis on emerging talent. A key venue during July's annual Dancing on the Edge festival (dancingontheedge.org), it also has a convivial licensed lounge on-site. (firehallartscentre.ca)

Shopping

Massy Books BOOKS

20 MAP P68, E4

A former pop-up favorite with a now-permanent Chinatown location, this delightful bookstore is lined with tall stacks of well-curated, mostly used titles. There's an impressively large selection of Indigenous-themed books, alongside good selections covering travel, history and literature – plus a bargain $1 cart outside. Love mysteries? Try finding the store's secret room, hidden behind a pushable bookcase door. (massybooks.com)

Eastside Flea MARKET

21 MAP P68, F4

A size upgrade from the market's previous venue has delivered a cavernous hall of hip arts and crafts-isans hawking everything from handmade chocolate bars to intricate jewelry and a humungous array of cool-ass vintage clothing. Give yourself plenty of time to hang out here; there's a pool table and retro arcade machines, plus food trucks and a long bar serving local craft beer. (eastsideflea.com)

John Fluevog Shoes

SHOES

22 MAP P68, C2

Like an art gallery for shoes, this alluringly cavernous store showcases the famed footwear of local designer Fluevog, whose men's and women's boots and brogues are what Doc Martens would have become if they'd stayed interesting and cutting-edge. Pick up that pair of thigh-hugging dominatrix boots you've always wanted or settle on some designer loafers that would make anyone walk tall. (fluevog.com)

Gore St Vintage

VINTAGE

23 MAP P68, E4

Traipse through this two-level, warehouse-like shop, where you'll find a top-tier selection of vintage tees, retro frocks and stonewashed denim, as well as a variety of vendors selling the latest vintage trends and styles.

Vintage Shopping

Gastown and Chinatown are studded with cool stores, but a growing number of vintage shops have also popped up on area side streets in recent years; you can check out several of them on Columbia St between Pender and Hastings.

Herschel Supply Co

FASHION & ACCESSORIES

24 MAP P68, B1

The friendly flagship store of this hot, Vancouver-based bags-and-accessories brand is a must-see for Herschel fans. Inside a beautifully restored, artwork-lined Gastown heritage building (check out the waterfront views from the back windows), you'll find a huge array of the company's signature daypacks, plus wallets, totes, pouches and recently added clothing lines. Give yourself plenty of perusing time; you're gonna need it. (herschel.com)

Brewing
Fresh Beer
Since
1994

Explore

Yaletown & Granville Island

These shoreline neighborhoods straddle tranquil False Creek, and both exemplify Vancouver's development in recent decades. Yaletown, a revitalized warehouse district, has become one of the chicest parts of the city, where waterfront parks, cool boutiques and posh urban patios draw crowds. Granville Island combines its industrial heritage with modern-day architecture, and is lauded as Vancouver's artisan capital, home to Western Canada's biggest public market.

The Short List

- ***Granville Island Public Market (p80)*** *Gathering some treats before catching a busker or two outside.*
- ***Vancouver Water Adventures (p90)*** *Sliding across False Creek on a guided kayak tour.*
- ***Vancouver Whitecaps (p92)*** *Joining the crowds for a BC Place pro-soccer game, face-painting optional.*

Getting There & Around

Bus 50 from downtown stops near Granville Island's entrance. Bus 10 stops on the south side of Granville Bridge, a five-minute stroll from the island.

The Canada Line from downtown stops at Yaletown-Roundhouse Station.

Yaletown has metered parking. Granville Island has free and paid parking.

Granville Island is accessible by mini-ferry from False Creek's north shore.

Yaletown & Granville Island Map on p86

Yaletown

Top Experience

Get Goodies at Granville Island Public Market

A foodie extravaganza specializing in deli treats and pyramids of shiny fruit and vegetables, this is one of North America's finest public markets. It's ideal for whiling away an afternoon snacking on goodies in the sun among the buskers outside or sheltering from the rain with a market tour. You'll also find side dishes of (admittedly inedible) arts and crafts.

MAP P87, G4

granvilleisland.com/public-market

Taste-Tripping

Come hungry: there are dozens of food stands to weave your way around at the market. Among the must-see vendors are **Oyama Sausage Company**, replete with hundreds of smoked sausages and cured meats; **Benton Brothers Fine Cheese**, with its full complement of amazing curdy goodies from British Columbia (BC) and around the world (look for anything by Farm House Natural Cheese from Agassiz, BC); and **Granville Island Tea Company** (Hawaiian rooibos recommended), with its tasting bar and more than 150 steep-tastic varieties to choose from.

Baked goodies also abound: abandon your diet at **Lee's Donuts** and **Siegel's Bagels**, where the naughty cheese-stuffed baked varieties are not to be missed. And don't worry: there's always room for a wafer-thin, album-sized 'cinnamon record' from **Stuart's Baked Goods**. French-themed **L'Epicerie Rotisserie & Gourmet Shop** has been a popular addition to the market. It sells vinegars, olive oils and delicious house-cooked dishes to go.

In the unlikely event you're still hungry, there's also a small international **food court**; avoid peak-time dining if you want to snag a table, and indulge in a good-value selection that runs from Mexican tacos to German sausages. And if you want to dive into some regional seasonal produce, there's a **farmers market** just outside the market building between June and October where you can sample BC-made booze.

Twin Bridges

If you're out enjoying the buskers on the market's waterfront exterior, you'll notice your False Creek view is sandwiched between two of Vancouver's most famous bridges. Opened in 1954, the ironwork **Granville Bridge** is the third version of this bridge to span the inlet

★ Top Tips

- Arrive early to sidestep the summer crowds, which peak in the afternoons.
- If you're driving, weekdays are the easiest times to find on-island parking.
- The food court is the island's best-value dining. But tables are scarce at peak times.
- Bird-watcher? Look for the cormorants nesting under the Granville Bridge span.

Take a Break

Just across from the Public Market, A Bread Affair (p90) serves excellent house-baked treats plus good-value gourmet sandwiches.

Fancy-free local favorite Tony's Fish & Oyster Cafe (p91) serves the island's best fish and chips; dine outside busy times since table spots are limited.

here. The more attractive art-deco **Burrard Bridge**, opened in 1932, is nearby. During the bridge's opening ceremony a floatplane was daringly piloted under its main deck.

Arts & Crafts

Once you've eaten your fill, take a look at some of the market's other stands. There's a cool arts-and-crafts focus here, especially among the collection of day vendors that dot the market and change every week.

Hand-knitted hats, hand-painted ceramics, framed art photography and quirky carvings make for excellent one-of-a-kind souvenirs. Further artisan stands are added to the roster in the run-up to Christmas, handy if you happen to be here at that time.

For more information on the sorts of day vendors that appear at the market, visit granvilleisland.com/directory.

Insider's Tour

If you're a hungry culinary fan, the delicious guided market walk organized by **Vancouver Foodie Tours** (foodietours.ca) is the way to go. This leisurely stomach-stuffer weaves around the vendors and includes several tasting stops that will quickly fill you up. It also caters to vegetarians if you mention this when you book.

The company runs friendly tasting tours in other parts of the city too, if you're keen to keep eating.

Burrard Bridge

The Island's Industrial Side

Many visitors spend their time on Granville Island at the Public Market end, nipping between the myriad shops and studios. But heading a few minutes along Johnston St offers some reminders of the time when this human-made peninsula (since it's joined to the mainland, it's not actually an island) was home to dozens of hard-toiling factories making everything from chains to iron hinges.

A whopping 760,000 cu meters of landfill was tipped into False Creek to create the island in the early 20th century, but almost all the reminders of its gritty first few years have been lost. Almost. The area's oldest tenant, **Ocean Concrete**, is a cement maker that began here in 1917 and now cranks out enough product to build a 10-story tower block every week. It also does a great job of being a good neighbor. A Vancouver Biennale initiative saw the company's six gigantic waterfront silos transformed into huge multicolored figures, while its annual April **open house** event is hotly anticipated by local families.

Continue along Johnston a little further and you'll come to a second monument to the past: a landmark **yellow dock crane** that's been preserved from the old days. Nip across to the waterfront here for a final 'hidden' Granville Island view: a string of large and comfy-looking **houseboats** that many Vancouverites wish they lived in.

Forgotten Past

The Public Market is the centerpiece of one of Canada's most impressive urban-regeneration projects – and the main reason this project has been so successful.

Built as a district for small factories in the early part of the last century, Granville Island – which has also been called Mud Island and Industrial Island over the years – had declined into a paint-peeled no-go area by the 1960s. But the abandoned sheds began attracting artists and theater groups by the 1970s, and the old buildings slowly started springing back to life with some much-needed repairs and upgrades.

Within a few years, new theaters, restaurants and studios had been built and the Public Market instantly became a popular anchor tenant.

One reason for the island's popularity? Only independent, one-of-a-kind businesses operate here.

Walking Tour

Granville Island Artisan Amble

Most visitors head straight for the Public Market, but locals know there's much more to check out on this artificial island, built up from sandbanks in False Creek more than a century ago. The former industrial sheds are now home to crafty shops, studio spaces and cool theaters, inviting leisurely waterfront exploration on sun-dappled days.

Walk Facts

Start Granville Island Licorice Parlour

End Granville Island Brewing

Length 1km; one hour

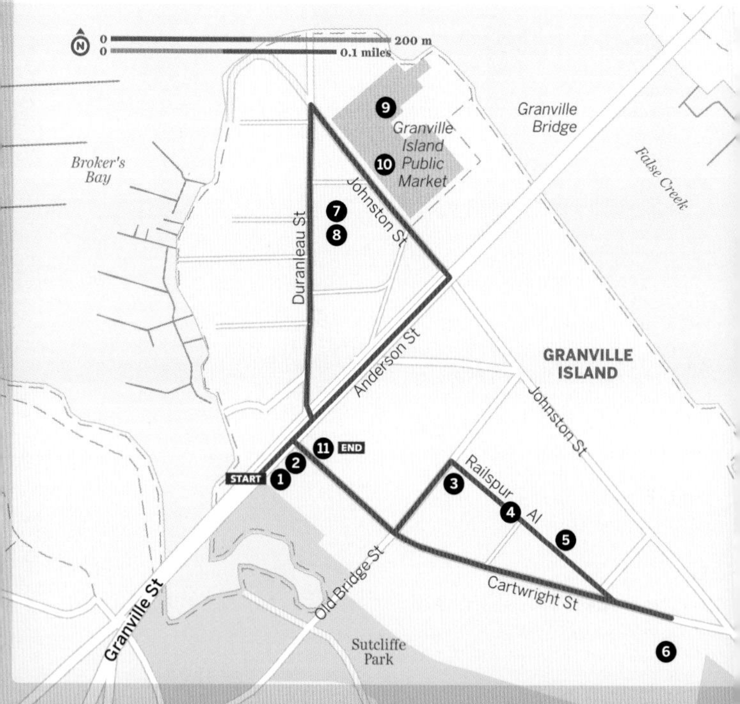

❶ Granville Island Licorice Parlour

Every stroll needs fuel, so drop into the friendly Granville Island Licorice Parlour (p95) for a hand-picked array of sweet and salty treats to keep you going.

❷ Kids Market

There's more than one market on the island and this one (p89) is fully focused on children. Look out for wooden toys, well-curated books and beady-eyed puppets.

❸ Liberty Distillery

Aim for happy hour at the saloon-like Liberty Distillery (p91) and you'll have the perfect pick-me-up. Don't overdo it, though: there's still plenty of walking to do.

❹ Railspur Alley

Starting just outside the distillery, this artisan-lined alleyway is a haven of creative businesses. Look out for inventive hats, eye-popping paintings and more.

❺ Artisan Sake Maker

In the middle of Railspur Alley, the Artisan Sake Maker (p92) is a welcoming little storefront where you can sample unique Vancouver-made libations. Consider buying a bottle to go as well.

❻ Kasama Chocolate

Sample small-batch, handcrafted, bean-to-bar chocolates (p95) created by four friends looking to share unique flavors from cacao pods sourced in the Philippines.

❼ Net Loft

A cluster (p95) of craft shops offers handcrafted keepsakes. At **Beadworks**, browse through an expansive collection of beads – from Swarovski crystals to bone beads – and make your own jewelry.

❽ Paper-Ya

The Net Loft's most popular store (p95) is home to an irresistible array of hip stationery, quirky books and must-have art prints.

❾ Public Market

Dominating the island's busy end, the market (p80) is a browser's paradise. But if you're hungry, you can also dive into tempting deli and bakery food stands.

❿ Lee's Donuts

Speaking of which, be sure to arrive at the market early to avoid long lines at Lee's Donuts. Serving up fresh, handmade classic doughnuts since 1979, Lee's has become a top spot for the sweet treat in the city.

⓫ Granville Island Brewing

Toast your wander in the taproom of one of Vancouver's oldest breweries (p89). Or take the guided tour, samples included.

A B C D

1 2 3 4 5 6

Nelson Park
Comox St
Barclay St
Jervis St
Pendrell St
Nelson St
Bute St
Davie St
Burnaby St
Thurlow St
Harwood St
Sunset Beach Park
Seaside Promenade
Beach Ave
Pacific St
Burrard St
Helmcken St
Hornby St
Howe St
False Creek Ferry
Granville St
Seymour St
Davie St
Burrard Bridge
Beach Ave
Drake St
Pacific St
Pacific Blvd
Seawall Trail
See Granville Island Enlargement
George Wainborn Park
David Lam Park
Granville St
7
Johnston St
Granville Island
False Creek Ferry
Aquabus Ferry
Cartwright St
False Creek
W 2nd Ave
Sutcliffe Park
The Mound
Spruce Harbour Marina
Island Park Walk
Fountain Way
W 4th Ave
Granville St
Charleson Park
Lamey's Mill Rd
W 6th Ave
Oak St
W 7th Ave
FAIRVIEW
Birch St
Alder St
Spruce St
W 8th Ave
Laurel St
W Broadway

For reviews see

Top Experiences	p80
Sights	p88
Eating	p90
Drinking	p91
Entertainment	p92
Shopping	p95

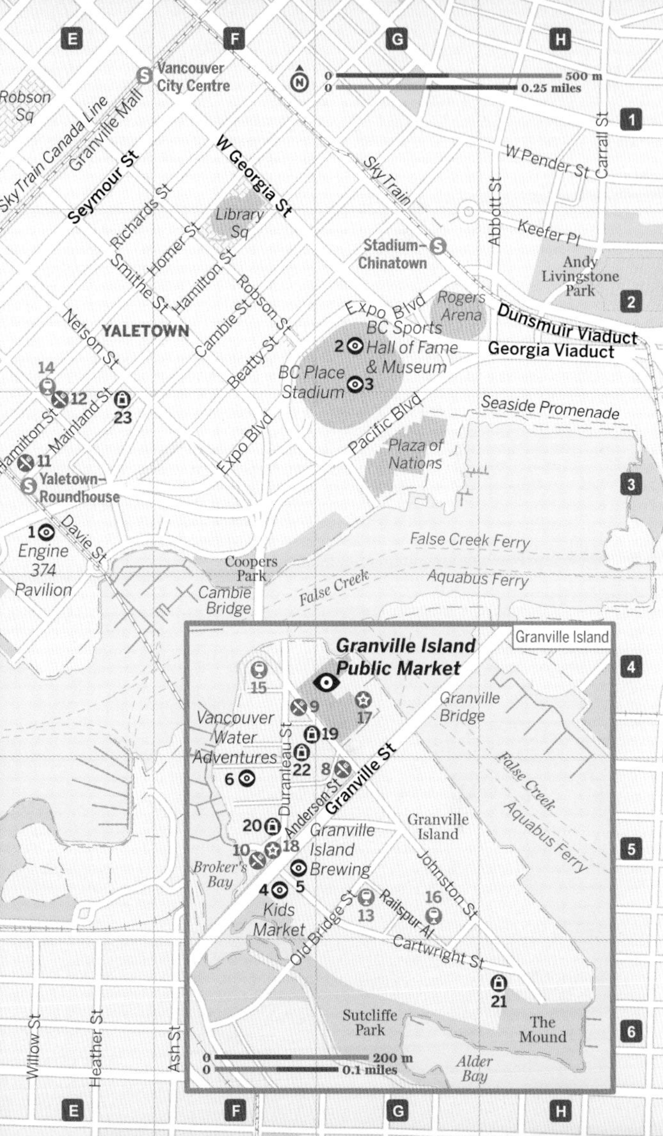

Vancouver City Centre
Robson Sq
SkyTrain Canada Line
Granville Mall
Seymour St
W Georgia St
Richards St
Library Sq
Homer St
Smithe St
Hamilton St
Robson St
Cambie St
Beatty St
Nelson St
YALETOWN
SkyTrain
W Pender St
Carrall St
Abbott St
Keefer Pl
Stadium-Chinatown
Andy Livingstone Park
Expo Blvd
Rogers Arena
Dunsmuir Viaduct
Georgia Viaduct
BC Sports Hall of Fame & Museum
BC Place Stadium
Mainland St
Seaside Promenade
Pacific Blvd
Plaza of Nations
Yaletown-Roundhouse
Davie St
Engine 374 Pavilion
False Creek Ferry
Aquabus Ferry
Coopers Park
Cambie Bridge
False Creek
Granville Island
Granville Island Public Market
Granville Bridge
Vancouver Water Adventures
Duranleau St
Anderson St
Granville St
Granville Island Brewing
Broker's Bay
Kids Market
Old Bridge St
Railspur Al
Johnston St
Cartwright St
Sutcliffe Park
The Mound
Alder Bay
Willow St
Heather St
Ash St
0 500 m
0 0.25 miles
0 200 m
0 0.1 miles

Sights

Engine 374 Pavilion

MUSEUM

1 MAP P87, E3

May 23, 1887, was an auspicious date for Vancouver. That's when Engine 374 pulled the very first transcontinental passenger train into the fledgling city, symbolically linking the country and kickstarting the eventual metropolis. Retired in 1945, the engine was restored and placed in this splendid pavilion after many years of neglect.

The friendly volunteers here will show you the best angle for snapping photos and share a few yesteryear railroading stories at the same time. (roundhouse.ca;)

BC Sports Hall of Fame & Museum

MUSEUM

2 MAP P87, G2

Inside BC Place Stadium, this expertly curated attraction showcases top BC athletes, both amateur and professional, with an intriguing array of galleries crammed with fascinating memorabilia. There are medals, trophies and vintage sports uniforms on display (judging by the size of their shirts, hockey players were much smaller in the past), plus tonnes of hands-on activities to tire the kids out. Don't miss the **Indigenous Sport Gallery**, covering everything from hockey to lacrosse to traditional Indigenous games. (bcsportshall.com)

Granville Island Brewing

Canada's Hero

The most poignant gallery at the BC Sports Hall of Fame & Museum is dedicated to national legend Terry Fox, the young cancer sufferer whose one-legged 1980 Marathon of Hope run across Canada ended after 143 days and 5373km, when the disease spread to his lungs.

Don't miss the memorial outside BC Place Stadium, created by Vancouver artist and writer Douglas Coupland, who also penned a celebrated book, *Terry*, in tribute to Fox. The statue is a series of running figures showing Fox in motion during his cross-country odyssey.

Every year since his death, fundraising runs have been held in Canada and around the world. The **Terry Fox Foundation** (terryfox.org) estimates these have raised more than $500 million for cancer research.

BC Place Stadium STADIUM

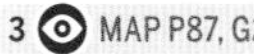

3 MAP P87, G2

Vancouver's main sports arena is home to two professional teams: the **BC Lions** Canadian Football League team and the **Vancouver Whitecaps** soccer team. Also used for international rugby sevens tournaments, major rock concerts and a wide array of consumer shows, the renovated stadium – with its huge, crown-like retractable roof – also hosted the opening and closing ceremonies for the 2010 Olympic and Paralympic Winter Games. (bcplace.com)

Kids Market MARKET

4 MAP P87, F5

A kaleidoscopic marketplace for the minis, Kids Market is a three-story kid-centric mall that features handcrafted toys, multi-level play spaces and interactive arcades for kids of all ages. If they need to cool off after hours of indoor play, Granville Island is home to the largest free outdoor water park in North America, **Granville Island Water Park**, just steps away. (kidsmarket.ca)

Granville Island Brewing BREWERY

5 MAP P87, F5

One of Canada's oldest microbreweries (established in 1984), GIB offers short tours during which smiling guides walk you through the tiny brewing nook. The brewery has grown exponentially since opening and most of its beers are now made off-site, although some excellent small-batch brews are still made here on the island. The tour concludes with some samples in the Taproom (p92). (gib.ca)

Vancouver Water Adventures

KAYAKING

6 

Headquartered on Granville Island, friendly Vancouver Water Adventures offers stand-up paddleboard (SUP) and single and double kayak rental, and guided boat tours, including the City & Seals Zodiak Tour (1½ hours, $69) and the Bowen Island Dinner & Sights Tour (three hours, $159). (vancouverwateradventures.com)

Eating

Go Fish

SEAFOOD $

7 

A short stroll westward along the seawall from the Granville Island entrance, this almost-too-popular seafood stand is one of the city's fave fish-and-chip joints, offering halibut, salmon and cod encased in crispy golden batter. The smashing fish tacos are also recommended, while changing daily specials – brought in by the nearby fishing boats – often include scallop burgers or ahi tuna sandwiches.

Island's Best Fest

It might feel like an invasion, but it's more accurate to call September's 11-day **Vancouver Fringe Festival** (vancouverfringe.com) an energetic occupation of Granville Island. The island's surfeit of theaters is well utilized, but shows are also staged at less conventional venues, from miniferries to pop-up street stages. Tickets are $12 to $15, but deals are plentiful and free shows are common: book ahead before you arrive.

Alimentaria Mexicana

MEXICAN $$

8 

A much-needed addition to Granville Island's culinary scene, this pan-Mexican cantina lures with its colorful corner patio, and appeases the taste buds with cauliflower tacos, *carnitas torta* with chorizo, and cinnamon-scented house-made churros. Accompany your meal with a chilled *cerveza* (beer) or smoky mezcal cocktail. Be sure to stop at the *mercado* out back for Mexican ceramics and dried spices. (alimentariamexicana.com)

A Bread Affair

BAKERY $

9 MAP P87, F4

A beloved Granville Island mainstay and must-visit for fans of great bread. Alongside its sandwich bar (French ham and Havarti recommended) and racks of fresh-baked loaves, there's an irresistible array of treats, from cookies to croissants to rich chocolate brownies. Don't miss the hearty apple-cheddar-walnut galette; it's enough to feed two (but that doesn't mean you have to share). (abreadaffair.com)

Tony's Fish & Oyster Cafe

SEAFOOD $$

10 MAP P87, F5

A chatty spot popular with both locals and visitors, this small, blue-checkered-tablecloth joint serves great fish and chips (cod, salmon or halibut), generously dolloped with house-made coleslaw and tartar sauce. The food is good value, and the menu goes beyond fish and seafood: the barbecue-sauced oyster burger is almost a local legend. Service is fast and friendly. (tonysfishandoystercafe.com)

MeeT

VEGAN $

11 MAP P87, E3

A hip vegan eatery that lures many carnivores with an array of meaty-seeming comfort-grub classics that emulate the flavors and textures of burgers, chicken and more.

The Yaletown branch of this Vancouver mini-chain is often busy with chatty diners – which can mean waiting for peak-time tables. If you're starving, go for the bulging crispy barbecue burger or butter 'chicken' poutine. (meetonmain.com)

Blue Water Cafe

SEAFOOD $$$

12 MAP P87, E3

Consistently recognized as Vancouver's best seafood restaurant, Blue Water is housed in a comfortably refurbished brick-and-beam warehouse, and serves up fine West Coast–inspired dining. The Raw Bar serves up fresh sushi and sashimi, and mains shine – try the freshly caught sablefish or yellowfin tuna.

Don't worry, carnivores: meaty dishes such as wagyu beef are also on offer here. Service here is perfect: warm, gracious and ever-friendly. Reservations are required. (bluewatercafe.net)

Drinking

Liberty Distillery

DISTILLERY

13 MAP P87, G5

Gaze through internal windows at the shiny, steampunk-like booze-making equipment when you visit this handsome saloon-style tasting room. It's not all about looks, though. During happy hour (3pm to 6pm and after 8pm Monday to Thursday), sample house-made vodka, gin varieties and several whiskeys, plus great $6 cocktails.

Tours are also available ($10, 11:30am and 1:30pm Saturday and Sunday). (thelibertydistillery.com)

Small Victory

COFFEE

14 MAP P87, E2

The kind of austere, granite-countered coffee shop you might not feel cool enough to enter, Small Victory is a favorite daytime hangout for hip Yaletowners. Sip your perfect cappuccino and standout flaky croissant (there's also an artful array of additional bakery treats) under the geometric wall-mounted artwork and you'll fit right in. (smallvictory.ca)

Tap & Barrel Bridges CRAFT BEER

15 MAP P87, F4

Vancouver-based chain Tap & Barrel is famous for its waterfront patios, and this location – in a historic yellow-hued industrial space once home to iconic restaurant Bridges – doesn't disappoint. A massive year-round veranda offers up Vancouver and water views, and the expansive drink menu includes more than 24 BC beers on tap (flights $13.50). Next-level comfort foods are also available. (tapandbarrel.com)

Artisan Sake Maker BREWERY

16 MAP P87, G5

Using locally grown rice, this tiny craft sake producer (the first of its kind in Canada) should be on everyone's Granville Island to-do list. Twinkle-eyed sake maker Masa Shiroki creates tempting tipples; you can dive in for a bargain $5 three-sake tasting. A visit is an eye-opener for many drinkers who think sake is a harsh beverage. Takeout bottles also available. (artisansakemaker.com)

Theater Tip

Granville Island is the heart of Vancouver's theater scene and hosts several stages. Savvy locals (and in-the-know visitors) save money on shows by checking the daily half-price deals at ticketstonight.ca.

Granville Island Brewing Taproom PUB

You can sample the company's (see 5 Map p87, F5) main beers in this often busy pub-style room, although most are now made in a far larger out-of-town facility. Of these, Cypress Honey Lager, Lions Winter Ale and False Creek Raspberry Ale are among the most popular. But the small-batch brews, made right here on the island, are even better; ask your server what's available. (gib.ca)

Entertainment

Vancouver Whitecaps SOCCER

Using BC Place Stadium (p89) (see 3 Map p87, G2) as its home, Vancouver's professional soccer team plays in North America's top-tier Major League Soccer (MLS). The Whitecaps' on-field fortunes have ebbed and flowed since they were promoted to the league in 2011, but they've been finding their feet (useful for soccer players) lately. Make time to buy a souvenir soccer shirt to impress everyone back home. (whitecapsfc.com;)

BC Lions FOOTBALL

Founded in 1954, the Lions (see 3 Map p87, G2) are Vancouver's team in the Canadian Football League (CFL), which is arguably more exciting than its US counterpart, the NFL. The team has had some decent showings lately, but it hasn't won the all-important Grey Cup since 2011. Tickets are easy to come by – unless the boys

BC Place Stadium (p89)

are laying into their arch enemies, the Calgary Stampeders. (bclions.com; 👪)

Granville Island Stage THEATER

17 MAP P87, G4

The Granville Island arm of Vancouver's leading theater company, this intimate, raked-seating venue is the perfect spot to feel really connected to the action on stage. Cutting-edge homegrown shows as well as new versions of established hits populate the season here, and you're close to several restaurants if you fancy a dinner-and-show night out. (artsclub.com)

Vancouver Theatresports COMEDY

18 MAP P87, F5

The city's most popular improv group stages energetic romps – sometimes connected to themes such as Tinder dating – at this purpose-built theater. Whatever the theme, the approach is the same: if you're sitting at one of the tables near the front, expect to be picked on. The late-night (11:15pm) shows are commendably ribald and probably not something to bring your parents to. (vtsl.com)

Vancouver's Brick-built Soho

Railway Foundation

Aesthetically unlike any other Vancouver neighborhood, Yaletown has a trendy warehouse-district appearance today because it was built on a foundation of grungy, working-class history.

Created almost entirely from red bricks, the area was crammed with railway sheds and goods warehouses in the late 1800s after the Canadian Pacific Railway (CPR) relocated its main Western Canada operation here from the BC interior town of Yale.

Neighborhood Decline

Along with the moniker, the workers brought something else with them: a tough-as-nails, hard-drinking approach that turned the waterfront area into one where the taverns usually served their liquor with a side order of fistfights.

But at least the rough-and-ready workers kept the area alive: when the rail operations were closed down a few decades later, Yaletown descended into a half-empty mass squat filled with homeless locals and marauding rats.

Yaletown Rises

But that wasn't the end of the story. When plans were drawn up for Vancouver to host the giant **Expo '86** world exposition, there were few areas of town with the requisite space – and the absence of other businesses. But Yaletown fit the bill. The area became part of the planned Expo grounds along the northern shoreline of False Creek, and it was cleared, refurbished and given a new lease on life.

Post-Expo Flourishing

New appreciation for Yaletown's historic character emerged during the summer-long Expo, making the district an ideal candidate for urban regeneration. Within a few years the old brick warehouses had been repaired, scrubbed clean and recolonized with a sparkling array of boutiques, fancy restaurants and swish bars – serving tipples that are a far cry from the punch-triggering beers that used to be downed here.

Shopping

Net Loft

MARKET

19 MAP P87, F4

Just across from the far busier Public Market is an indoor array of creative boutiques. Highlight stores include arts-and-crafty Paper-Ya, the cave-like Granville Island Hat Shop and the Wickaninnish Gallery, where Indigenous designs adorn everything from jewelry to framed prints to cool water bottles.

Karen Cooper Gallery

ART

20 MAP P87, F5

You'll feel as though you've entered a tranquil forest clearing when you open the door of this delightful nature-themed photography gallery. Cooper's striking work focuses on BC's jaw-dropping wild beauty, from coniferous trees to grizzly bears. Take your time and don't be surprised if you fall in love with a handsome image of a bald eagle perched on a mountain tree. (karencoopergallery.com)

Kasama Chocolate

FOOD

21 MAP P87, H6

For a take-home sweet treat, head to Kasama Chocolate for bean-to-bar chocolate and truffles made using unusual ingredients. The durian chocolate bar is made from the namesake pungent tropical fruit found only in the southern Philippines. (kasamachocolate.com)

Paper-Ya

ARTS & CRAFTS

22 MAP P87, F4

A magnet for slavering stationery fetishists, this store's treasure trove of trinkets ranges from natty pens to traditional *washi* paper. It's not all writing-related ephemera, though. Whoever does the buying curates an eclectic roster of hard-to-resist goodies that can include cool journals, quirky books and cute greeting cards emblazoned with everything from cats to owls. (paper-ya.com)

Granville Island Licorice Parlour

FOOD

A satellite branch of Commercial Dr's popular candy store, this sweet-tooth pilgrimage spot (see 4 Map p87, F5) serves up dozens of jars of serious licorice (anyone for salty *salmiak* from Scandinavia?) alongside a kaleidoscopic array of sweeties and bonbons such as jelly babies and saltwater taffy. There are also lots of gelatin-free and gluten-free options, plus a super-cool sideline in brightly colored Hula Hoops.

Fine Finds

FASHION & ACCESSORIES

23 MAP P87, E3

Browse the carefully curated independent labels at this locally owned women's fashion boutique, and try not to take everything home. The work of local jewelry designers and artists is showcased here, and eco-friendly gifts make for the perfect keepsakes. (finefindsboutique.com)

Walking Tour

Commercial Drive Beer & Bites

One of Vancouver's most colorful and culturally rich neighborhoods, the Drive is lined with great places to hang with the locals on restaurant patios and in chatty bars, coffee shops and eclectic boutiques. It's also easy to get to and explore: a simple SkyTrain hop from downtown, the street unfolds just steps from the bustling Commercial-Broadway station.

Getting There

Expo SkyTrain line from downtown to Commercial-Broadway station.

99B-Line express and regular bus 9 both stop at the intersection of Broadway and Commercial Dr.

❶ St Augustine's

Walk north from the SkyTrain station and you'll soon reach this busy **pub** (staugustinesvancouver.com), complete with dozens of temping craft beers from BC and beyond.

❷ Prado

Sober up with the hip locals at **Prado** (pradocafe.co). It's one of many Drive coffee shops, testament to a rich java scene launched by Italian immigrants in the 1950s.

❸ Craft Maison

If you're looking for unique gifts and keepsakes, this souvenir shop is sure to impress. You'll only find handmade products here, ranging from stylish steampunk lamps to wooden board games and chess sets. Items are crafted by professional artisans and each modern piece is a standout selection.

❹ Mintage

The Commercial Dr location of this valued vintage shop specializes in offering hand-selected vintage fashion pieces and one-of-a-kind finds. Pick up vintage dresses and tees and unique accessories from a wide variety of items found in this streetside treasure trove, housed in a 280-sq-meter space.

❺ Grandview Park

Time for a break? Sit on the grass at Grandview Park while eyeballing the visuals to the north (craggy-topped peaks) and west (twinkling downtown towers).

❻ Havana

Hit **Havana** (havanavancouver.com) – the hottest patio on the Drive – and brunch on Cuban cuisine and some boozy bevies (it's 12 o'clock somewhere).

❼ Lunch Lady

Lunch Lady (thelunchlady.ca) is not your average *pho* joint: the Vietnamese street eats served here caught the attention of the late Anthony Bourdain.

❽ East Van Brewing Company

Conclude your libation-loving wander with a tasting flight at **East Van Brewing Company** (eastvanbrewing.com), a local microbrewery favorite.

WWW.DRAGONBOATBC.CA
RioTintoAlcan

Explore

Main Street

Formerly faded and gritty, the skinny-jeaned heart of Vancouver's hipster scene is now its coolest 'hood, with many of its best independent shops, global restaurants and hip bars. A great place to meet locals away from the city center, this area is developing rapidly. And that includes the Olympic Village, a waterfront neighborhood that's always adding new drink and dine options.

The Short List

- ***Regional Assembly of Text (p109)*** *Composing pithy missives to your loved one on vintage typewriters at the legendary monthly letter-writing club.*
- ***Anh & Chi (p104)*** *Dining on delightful contemporary Vietnamese dishes (and a glass or three of house-made punch) at this vibrant eatery.*
- ***Brassneck Brewery (p105)*** *Downing a Passive Aggressive pale ale at Vancouver's favorite neighborhood microbrewery.*
- ***Red Cat Records (p109)*** *Browsing the racks, buying local gig tickets and finally finding that vintage vinyl you've been looking for.*

Getting There & Around

Bus 3 runs the length of Main St in both directions.

SkyTrain connects to bus 3 services at Main St-Science World Station. If you're on the Canada Line, alight at Broadway-City Hall Station and take the 99B-Line bus along Broadway to Main St.

There's limited metered parking on Main St, with side-street parking the further south you drive.

Main Street Map on p102

ARCHITECT BRUNO FRESCHI

Waterfront, Science World (p100) SONGQUAN DENG/SHUTTERSTOCK ©

Top Experience

Entertain the Entire Family at Science World

Vancouver's landmark geodesic dome isn't just a shiny shoreline bauble; it's also home to the city's most popular family-friendly attraction. Teeming with hands-on exhibits, engaging galleries, an eye-popping large-format movie theater and much more, it's the kind of attraction you plan to cover quickly but find yourself still exploring three hours later.

MAP P102, B1

scienceworld.ca

Ground-Floor Fun

Start by letting your kids loose on the lower level's **Puzzles & Illusions** gallery, a tactile array of activities from wobble rings to whisper dishes. It's the kind of place where your children will show you just how much smarter they are than you.

Reward their braininess by paying extra ($8) for **Birdly**, a virtual-reality solo flight over a tower-forested city. Nearby, take a seat and check out the schedule of live science demonstrations on the **Centre Stage**.

Upstairs Action

Next, wander up to the 2nd level. It's circled by themed galleries bristling with hands-on action, including the nature-flavored **Sara Stern Gallery** (with fossils, taxidermy and live critters) and the brilliant **BodyWorks**, exploring the engineering marvels of the human body, with every fascinating function fully explained. This level is where you'll likely spend much of your time; there's a huge array of imaginative exhibits here and your kids will become fully engaged in many of the options.

Playing Outside

If the weather's fine, make sure you save time for the outdoor **Ken Spencer Science Park**. Focused on sustainable communities, it's a quirky collection of climbing frames, rugged interactive games and stage demonstrations, plus a coop full of beady-eyed, brightly plumed chickens. It's like a playground on steroids, and many kids will happily spend hours here if you let them.

But if it's time to leave, you can entice them away with a visit to Science World's popular gift shop, where excellent educational toys await.

★ Top Tips

- Check the times of Centre Stage shows when you arrive and plan your visit accordingly.
- After Dark adult evenings are very popular; book ahead online before you arrive.
- Add a mini-ferry cruise to your Science World day out; vessels docks nearby from Yaletown, Granville Island and other False Creek destinations.

✕ Take a Break

For a great finale to your family day out, head to Earnest Ice Cream (p103) for sit-down treats.

If dinner calls, walk around the False Creek shoreline to Tap & Barrel (p105), waterfront patio views included.

Science World
False Creek
Main Street–Science World
Thornton Park
Pacific Central Station
500 m
0.25 miles
Terminal Ave
Olympic Village
MOUNT PLEASANT
Industrial Ave
Great Northern Way
W 1st Ave
E 1st Ave
W 2nd Ave
E 2nd Ave
W 3rd Ave
E 3rd Ave
W 4th Ave
E 4th Ave
W 5th Ave
E 5th Ave
W 6th Ave
E 6th Ave
33 Acres Brewing Company
Main Street Brewing
W 7th Ave
E 7th Ave
Jonathan Rogers Park
Guelph Park
W 8th Ave
E 8th Ave
W Broadway
E Broadway
W 10th Ave
E 10th Ave
W 11th Ave
E 11th Ave
W 12th Ave
E 12th Ave
W 13th Ave
E 13th Ave
W 14th Ave
E 14th Ave
W 15th Ave
E 15th Ave
W 16th Ave
E 16th Ave
W 17th Ave
E 17th Ave
W 18th Ave
E 18th Ave
SOUTH MAIN (SOMA)
W 19th Ave
E 19th Ave
W 20th Ave
E 20th Ave
W 21st Ave
E 21st Ave
W 22nd Ave
E 22nd Ave
W 23rd Ave
E 23rd Ave
E 24th Ave
W King Edward Ave
E King Edward Ave
E 26th Ave
E 27th Ave
E 28th Ave
Québec St
Main St
Alberta St
Columbia St
Ontario St
Scotia St
Carolina St
Guelph St
St George St
Fraser St
Prince Albert St
Manitoba St
Prince Edward St
Kingsway
Sophia St
Yukon St
Peveril Ave
Talisman St

For reviews see

Top Experiences	p100
Sights	p103
Eating	p103
Drinking	p105
Entertainment	p109
Shopping	p109

Sights

Olympic Village

AREA

1 MAP P102, B1

Built as the home for 2800 athletes during the 2010 Olympic and Paralympic Winter Games, this glassy waterfront development became the city's newest neighborhood once the sporting types went home. New shops, bars and restaurants – plus some cool public art – have made this an increasingly happening area. Worth a look on your seawall stroll.

Eating

Federal Store

CAFE $

2 MAP P102, B3

Revitalizing an old mom-and-pop corner store into a funky little community cafe, this warmly welcoming checker-floored charmer serves coffee, light breakfasts and delicious lunch sandwiches (go for the juicy porchetta).

Among the bakery treats, a boutique array of artisan groceries and knickknacks, and lots of chatty locals, you'll feel like you're in the heart of the neighborhood. (federalstore.ca)

Earnest Ice Cream

ICE CREAM $

3 MAP P102, B2

The Olympic Village branch of this popular artisan ice-cream shop is tucked into a redbrick former warehouse building.

There's typically a dozen or so flavors, split between regulars including salted caramel and whiskey hazelnut, and seasonals such as the utterly delicious lemon

The Birds' sculpture, Olympic Plaza

Street-Art Murals

Explore the city through an artistic lens with a self-guided tour of the **Vancouver Mural Festival** (vanmuralfest.ca) – a stunning showcase of more than 300 outdoor murals and public art displays created by local and international artists.

The murals are found in 11 neighborhoods throughout the city. If you're in town in August, look out for the 10-day celebration that goes by the same name, featuring pop-up events, new murals and an epic Mount Pleasant street party.

poppy seed. All are available in cone or cup form – plus naughty to-go pint jars. (earnesticecream.com)

Trafiq

CAFE $

4 MAP P102, B6

This sometimes clamorously busy French-influenced bakery-cafe is a lunchtime magnet with its quesadillas, house-made soups and bulging grilled sandwiches (California club on cranberry pecan recommended).

But the best time to come is off peak, when you can snag a table and take on one of the large, belly-busting cake slabs. Miss the salted-caramel slice at your peril. (trafiq.ca)

Toshi Sushi

JAPANESE $

5 MAP P102, B4

There are no reservations and the place is tiny, but this unassuming sushi joint just off Main is the best place in the neighborhood for Japanese dining. Expect to line up (try to arrive outside peak time) before tucking into outstanding fresh-made dragon rolls, crunchy tempura and succulent sashimi platters; order a selection and everyone at the table will be delighted.

Anh & Chi

VIETNAMESE $$

6 MAP P102, B4

You'll find warm and solicitous service at this delightful contemporary Vietnamese restaurant whose authentic, perfectly prepared dishes are a must for local foodies. Not sure what to order? Check out the menu's 'bucket list' dishes, including the highly recommended prawn-and-pork-packed crunchy crepe.

Reservations are not accepted and waits here can be long; consider mid-afternoon weekday dining instead. (anhandchi.com)

Acorn

VEGETARIAN $$

7 MAP P102, B6

One of Vancouver's hottest vegetarian restaurants – hence the sometimes long wait for tables – the Acorn is ideal for those craving something more inventive than mung-bean soup. Consider seasonal, artfully presented treats such as beer-battered haloumi or vanilla-almond-beet cake, and stick around at night: the bar serves until midnight if you need to pull up a stool and set the world to rights. (theacornrestaurant.ca)

Sula Indian Restaurant
SOUTH INDIAN $$

8 MAP P102, B6

Savory South Indian–inspired cuisine featuring traditional roasted-coconut-based curries, tangy Mangalorean fish curries and distinctive Mumbai street foods are served here, and the warm and welcoming space nods to the owners' childhood roots. (sulaindianrestaurant.com)

Fable Diner
DINER $$

9 MAP P102, B3

Transforming a former greasy spoon in the landmark Lee Building into a casual satellite of Fable's popular Kitsilano restaurant, this hipster diner is a favorite Mount Pleasant hangout.

Snag a window booth or swivel chair at the kitchen-facing counter and dive into elevated all-day breakfasts and comfort grub, including the smashing roast duck and kimchi pancake. (fablediner.com)

Fish Counter
SEAFOOD $$

10 MAP P102, B5

Serving Main's best fish and chips, this busy spot combines a seafood wet counter and a bustling fry operation. Order from the cashier, snag a spot at the stand-up table inside or the sit-down benches outside and wait to be called.

Battered halibut and cod are popular, but the standout is the wild salmon, served with fries and a mound of 'slaw. (thefishcounter.ca)

Tap & Barrel
NORTHWESTERN US $$

11 MAP P102, B1

In the heart of Olympic Village, this popular neighborhood haunt serves gourmet comfort nosh such as Cajun chicken burgers and pineapple-and-pulled-pork pizzas. In summer it's all about the views from the expansive, mountain-facing waterfront patio (the area's best alfresco dining). Add some BC beer or wine and you'll have to be forcibly removed at the end of the night. (tapandbarrel.com)

Drinking

Brassneck Brewery
MICROBREWERY

12 MAP P102, B2

A beloved Vancouver microbrewery, Brassneck has a small, wood-lined tasting room. Peruse the ever-changing chalkboard of intriguing libations with names such as Pinky Promise, Silent Treatment and Faux Naive, or start with a delicious, highly accessible Passive Aggressive dry-hopped pale ale.

It's often hard to find a seat here, so consider a weekday afternoon visit for a four-glass tasting flight ($8). (brassneck.ca)

Key Party

BAR

13 MAP P102, B3

Walk through the doorway of a fake storefront that looks like an accountancy office and you'll find yourself in a candlelit, boudoir-red speakeasy dominated by a dramatic mural of frolicking women and animals.

Arrive early to avoid the queues, then fully explore the entertaining cocktail program (kir royale jello shooters included). (keyparty.ca)

Shameful Tiki Room

BAR

14 MAP P102, B6

This windowless snug instantly transports you to a Polynesian beach. The lighting – including glowing puffer-fish lampshades – is permanently set to dusk and the walls are lined with tiki masks and rattan coverings under a straw-shrouded ceiling. But it's the drinks that rock: seriously well-crafted classics from zombies to blue Hawaiis to a four-person volcano bowl (don't forget to share it). (shamefultikiroom.com)

49th Parallel Coffee

COFFEE

15 MAP P102, B4

Main's most popular coffeehouse, this large, brick-lined hangout is routinely crammed with locals, and its alfresco side-street patio is particularly popular in the summer.

It roasts its own coffee, so the quality is high and you can also face-plant into a full selection of lovely Lucky's doughnuts (apple-bacon fritter recommended), calling your name from their glass cabinet near the entrance. (49thcoffee.com)

Brewery Creek

Mainland Brewery, Red Star Brewery, San Francisco Brewery and, of course, Vancouver Brewery. The names of the city's long-gone beer producers recall a time when Brewery Creek (an area radiating from Main St around 7th Ave) concocted the suds quaffed by many ale-loving Vancouverites. The area was named after a fast-moving creek that once powered water wheels at several area breweries. But after decades of consolidation, the neighborhood's last brewery closed in the 1950s.

That wasn't the end of the story, though. In recent years, Vancouver's latter-day craft-brewing renaissance has seen several new producers open in this area, from **Main Street Brewing** (mainstreetbeer.ca) to **33 Acres Brewing** (33acresbrewing.com). Wondering where to start? Slake your thirst at local favorite Brassneck Brewery (p105).

Lucky's doughnut, 49th Parallel Coffee

Narrow Lounge

BAR

16 MAP P102, B2

Enter through the doorway on 3rd Ave – the red light tells you if it's open or not – then descend the graffiti-lined stairway into one of Vancouver's coolest small bars. Little bigger than a train carriage and lined with taxidermy and junk-shop pictures, it's an atmospheric nook where it always feels like 2am. In summer, try the hidden alfresco bar out back. (narrow lounge.com)

Sing Sing Beer Bar

BAR

17 MAP P102, B3

This bright, white-walled, plant-accented bar would look at home on a Singapore side street. Snag a communal table and dive into the 20 or so BC craft-beer taps (often including lesser-known libations from celebrated microbreweries such as Twin Sails and Fuggles & Warlock). Food-wise, there's an unusual combination of pizzas and hearty *pho* bowls on the menu. (singsingbeerbar.com)

Gene Cafe

COFFEE

18 MAP P102, B3

Colonizing a flatiron wedge of bare concrete floors and oversized windows, Gene is like a living-room hangout for many locals, especially if they manage to monopolize one of the three tiny tables overlooking Main and Kingsway.

Coffee is artfully prepared and the menu has expanded to include flake-tastic croissants

Vancouver's Summer Fair

One annual family-friendly Vancouver event is still going strong after more than a century. Launched in 1912, the **Pacific National Exhibition** (pne.ca) – known simply as the PNE by locals – is an August tradition for generations of Vancouverites. It's held in East Vancouver; you can reach it by hopping aboard bus 14 at the intersection of Main and Hastings Sts.

Planning Your Visit

Arrive as close to opening time as you can. This helps beat the crowds but also gives you the chance to see as much as possible. The site is crammed with **exhibition halls** and **arenas**; take time to check out the **market halls** lined with vendors selling 'miracle' made-for-TV products. Then head to the **livestock barns**; the PNE is an important agricultural show for BC farmers, and these barns are lined with prize horses, cows, goats and sheep.

Daily Shows

Included with your admission (typically around $18 but cheaper if you buy via the PNE website) is a wide array of other performances running all day. In recent years, these have included **magician shows**, **motorcycle stunts** and the **SuperDogs**. There's also **live music** on alfresco stages throughout the day, especially in the evening, with nostalgic acts such as Foreigner and Smokey Robinson adding to the party atmosphere in recent years.

Midway Shenanigans

The site's **Playland fairground** offers more than 50 rides, from dodgems to horror houses, but the top lure for thrill-seekers is the 1950s-built wooden **roller coaster**. Coaster aficionados from across North America frequently eulogize this scream-triggering boneshaker, which reaches speeds of up to 75km/h (47mph).

Food-a-Paloozza

This is also the one time of year when Vancouverites forget about their yoga-and-rice-cakes regimen, happily loosening their pants and stuffing themselves silly. The midway is jam-packed with indulgent treats from **deep-fried ice-cream** to **half-meter-long hot dogs**. And don't miss the event's biggest diet-defying tradition: warm bags of sugar-coated **mini doughnuts**.

(gooey chocolate variety recommended), plus Aussie-style meat pies and all-day breakfast wraps. (genecoffeebar.ca)

Entertainment

Fox Cabaret LIVE MUSIC

One of North America's last remaining porn cinemas has been transformed (and fully pressure-washed) into a brilliantly eclectic independent nightlife venue, ditching the dodgy flicks in favor of live bands, rib-tickling comedy, and Saturday-night dance fests with disco or '90s themes (see 13 Map p102, B3). Check the online calendar; there's always something different on stage in this narrow, high-ceilinged venue. (foxcabaret.com)

BMO Theatre Centre THEATER

19 MAP P102, A1

The studio venue of the city's Arts Club theater empire hosts more challenging and intimate productions in a space that's cleverly and sometimes dramatically reconfigured for each show. There are often three or four productions per season, as well as on-stage readings (typically free) of new works in progress; check the Arts Club website for information on these. (artsclub.com)

Biltmore Cabaret LIVE MUSIC

20 MAP P102, C3

One of Vancouver's favorite alt venues, the intimate Biltmore is a firm fixture on the local indie scene. A low-ceilinged, good-vibe spot to mosh to local and touring musicians, it also has regular event nights; check the online calendar for upcoming happenings, including trivia nights and stand-up comedy shows. (biltmorecabaret.com)

Shopping

Red Cat Records MUSIC

21 MAP P102, B6

Arguably Vancouver's coolest record store and certainly the only one named after a much-missed cat... There's a brilliantly curated collection of new and used vinyl and CDs, and it's co-owned by musicians; ask them for tips on where to see great local acts such as Loscil and Nick Krgovich, or peruse the huge list of shows in the window. (redcat.ca)

Regional Assembly of Text ARTS & CRAFTS

22 MAP P102, B6

This ironic antidote to the digital age lures ink-stained locals with its journals, handmade pencil boxes and T-shirts printed with typewriter motifs. Check out the tiny gallery under the stairs, showcasing global zines, and don't miss the monthly Letter Writing Club (7pm, first Thursday of every month), where you can hammer on vintage typewriters, crafting erudite missives to far-away loved ones. (assemblyoftext.com)

Urban Source

ARTS & CRAFTS

23 MAP P102, B4

From used postcards and insect rubber stamps to ladybug stickers and map pages from old books, this brilliant store offers a highly eclectic, ever-changing array of reclaimed materials and alternative arts-and-crafts supplies to a loyal band of locals. In this browser's paradise you'll suddenly be inspired to make an oversized pterodactyl model from glitter and discarded cassette tapes. (urban-source.ca;)

Front & Company

CLOTHING, ACCESSORIES

24 MAP P102, B5

You could easily spend a couple of hours perusing the new and vintage clothing in the main space of Front & Company, which colonizes a row of storefronts along Main and threatens to become a hipster department store in the process.

There are also knowingly cool housewares and must-have gifts and accessories (anyone for manga nightlights and unicorn ice trays?). (frontandcompany.ca)

Neptoon Records

MUSIC

25 MAP P102, B5

Vancouver's oldest independent record store is still a major lure for music fans, with its *High Fidelity* ambience and time-capsule feel. But it's not resting on its laurels: you'll find a well-priced array of new and used vinyl and CDs, plus some serious help with

Jeremy Allingham, Car Free Day, Neptoon Records

MICHAEL WHEATLEY/ALAMY STOCK PHOTO ©

finding that obscure Mighty Wah! recording you've been looking for. (neptoon.com)

Mintage Mall

VINTAGE

26 MAP P102, B3

Comprising seven super-cool vintage vendors offering everything from 1970s outfits (at Thirteen Moons) to antique taxidermy (Salamander Salt Curio), this eclectic, labyrinthine upstairs 'mall' is one of the best ways to spend an hour in Mount Pleasant.

Don't miss the ever-changing pop-up unit. Add a tarot reading to keep things lively and check out the mall's Instagram account for after-hours events.

Turnabout Luxury Resale

VINTAGE

27 MAP P102, B4

This well-stocked shop is stuffed with curated and consignment luxury fashions, footwear and finds. Since 1978, this has been the place to find those seemingly unattainable brand-name items (yes, even those Prada pumps) at an affordable price. (turnabout.com)

Main's Best Fest

If you make it to the neighborhood's annual **Car Free Day** (carfreevancouver.org), staged along Main St from the Broadway intersection for at least 30 blocks, you'll realize there's much more diversity in this area than you thought. Taking over the streets for this family-friendly community event are live music, craft stalls, steaming food stands, and a highly convivial atmosphere that makes for a brilliant party-like afternoon with the locals. Check the website for event dates.

Pulpfiction Books

BOOKS

28 MAP P102, B3

One of the city's best used-book stores (there are also plenty of new tomes in the front room), this is the ideal haunt for the kind of serious browsing where you forget what time it is. You'll find good literature and sci-fi sections, as well as a travel area at the back for planning your next big trip. (pulpfictionbooksvancouver.com)

Explore

Fairview & South Granville

Combining the boutiques and restaurants of well-to-do South Granville with Fairview's busy Broadway thoroughfare and cozy Cambie Village, this part of Vancouver has something for everyone. It's a great spot to scratch beneath the city's surface and meet the locals where they live, shop and socialize. Green-thumbed visitors should also save time for some top-notch park and garden attractions in the area.

The Short List

- ***Bloedel Conservatory (p120)*** *Spotting rainbow-hued tropical birds, then discovering the surrounding park's panoramic city views.*
- ***Pacific Arts Market (p126)*** *Perusing the work of dozens of regional artists and artisans in this shared gallery space.*
- ***Vij's (p122)*** *Face-planting into Vancouver's (and maybe Canada's) finest Indian food; lamb popsicles included.*

Getting There & Around

Cambie Village's shopping and dining area is sandwiched between the Canada Line SkyTrain stations at Broadway-City Hall and King Edward. The rest of Fairview also radiates along Broadway from the Broadway-City Hall station.

Bus 15 runs along Cambie St; bus 10 along South Granville. The two streets are linked along Broadway by buses 9 and 99B-Line express.

There is metered parking on Cambie and South Granville.

Fairview & South Granville Map on p118

Bloedel Conservatory (p120) NOAH SAUVE/SHUTTERSTOCK ©

Top Experience

Bask in the Blooms at VanDusen Botanical Garden

MAP P119, B8

vandusengarden.org

Vancouver's favorite manicured green space is a delightful confection of verdant walkways fringed by local and exotic flora. Over 500 varietals of plants bloom here, from temperate trees to tropical flowers, pleasing both people and pollinators.

Plant Life

Opened in 1975, this 22-hectare green-thumbed wonderland is home to more than 250,000 plants representing some of the world's most distinctive growing regions. You'll find trees, shrubs, flowers, succulents and more from across Canada, the Mediterranean, South Africa and the Himalayas, many of them identified with little plaques near their roots.

There's almost always something in bloom here; if you're lucky, that might include the eye-popping **Rhododendron Walk** or the neon-yellow, tunnel-like **Laburnum Walk**. Pick up a self-guided tour sheet from the front desk for seasonal tips on what to see, or time your visit for a free guided tour.

Wildlife

It's not just humans who are hooked by this sparkling nature swathe; this is also a wildlife haven. Look out for turtles, herons and a variety of ducks in and around the main lake. You might also see owls, bats, raccoons or the occasional coyote in quiet corners. But birds are the main critters here. There are regular guided **bird walks** (included with admission), and highlights that lure visiting camera lenses include eagles, hummingbirds and woodpeckers.

Elizabethan Maze

Grown from more than 3000 pyramidal cedars, VanDusen's giggle-triggering traditional maze is the perfect spot to tire out your kids.

Alternatively, just send them in there alone while you take a break outside. Now more than 25 years old, the maze has just the right combination of confusing dead-ends and gratifying solvability to give most visitors an entertaining diversion.

★ Top Tips

- Quiz the docents. These wandering volunteers are full of knowledge about the plants and wildlife you'll spot during your visit.
- VanDusen is also studded with artworks; see how many you can find along the walkways.
- The **Garden Shop** is stuffed with excellent books and gifts for the botanically inclined.
- VanDusen's **Festival of Lights** is a Christmas tradition, with thousands of twinkling bulbs dotting the gardens.

✕ Take a Break

Head to VanDusen's **Garden Cafe** (trufflesfinefoods.com) for light lunch options and fair-trade coffee. Try for a patio table facing the garden.

Walking Tour

South Granville Stroll

A stretch of stylish shops and independent galleries makes this vibrant, upscale shopping district worth the trek. South Granville is home to heritage buildings and casual cafes intermixed with modern boutiques and high-end eateries. Massive murals add charm, and colorful open-air plazas invite a rest stop after an afternoon spent shopping and snacking along one of the city's trendiest streets.

Walk Facts

Start Paul's Omelettery

End Small Victory

Length 1.5km; one hour

❶ Paul's Omelettery

On Granville St, just past the southern end of the bridge, Paul's Omelettery (p121) is a legend among breakfast-loving locals. Dive into a heaping plateful and then work it off as you speed-walk uphill.

❷ Pacific Arts Market

Take the stairs to this friendly, well-hidden, 2nd-floor market (p126) and you'll discover a cornucopia of arts and crafts created by an ever-changing array of BC creative types. Looking for special souvenirs? You'll find everything from painted ceramics to handmade chocolate bars here.

❸ Purdys Chocolates

If you didn't find the chocolate you wanted at the market, drop by Purdys (p127), a historic, home-grown confectionary chain with purple-hued shops throughout the region. Pick up some treats for later or an ice-cream bar for the road.

❹ Mazahr Lebanese Kitchen

You'll have spotted some enticing restaurants on your walk, covering cuisines from Japanese to Indian. But if you're starting to seriously mull your dinner options, check out the menu of meze, wine and happy-hour specials at Mazahr (p123).

❺ Stanley Theatre

Just around the corner, this handsome heritage theater (p125) is one of the city's most popular performance venues. Check to see what's on, and consider booking tickets for an evening show.

❻ Bacci's

This stretch of South Granville is lined on both sides with tempting boutiques, but this well-curated store (p127) should be on everyone's shopping list. Check out its funky homewares and trendy fashions.

❼ Meinhardt Fine Foods

Not far from the area's posh Shaughnessy neighborhood, Meinhardt (p127) is a high-end Vancouver deli and grocery store. Explore the aisles of fancy goods and tempting treats.

❽ Small Victory

Rest your weary feet after all that walking with a stop at Small Victory (p123), a quaint street-side cafe. Sip a coffee while snacking on a sweet or savory freshly baked treat, and people-watch from your seat.

Charleson Park
Lamey's Mill Rd
W 5th Ave
W 6th Ave
W 7th Ave
W 8th Ave
W Broadway
W 10th Ave
W 11th Ave
W 12th Ave
W 13th Ave
W 14th Ave
W 15th Ave
W 16th Ave
W 17th Ave
W 18th Ave
W 19th Ave
W 20th Ave
Granville St
Fir St
Hemlock St
Birch St
Alder St
Spruce St
Oak St
Laurel St
Willow St
Heather St
Ash St
Cambie St
Yukon St
Alberta St
Columbia St
Manitoba St
Jonathan Rogers Park
Vancouver General Hospital
City Hall
Broadway–City Hall
SkyTrain Canada Line
SOUTH GRANVILLE
SHAUGHNESSY
Shaughnessy Park
Douglas Park
McRae Ave
Tecumseh Ave
Wolfe Ave
Osler St
Matthews Ave
Angus Dr
Marpole Ave
500 m
0.25 miles

For reviews see

Top Experiences	p114
Sights	p120
Eating	p121
Drinking	p123
Entertainment	p125
Shopping	p126

A B C D E F
5 6 7 8

Balfour Ave
W 21st Ave
W 22nd Ave
W 23rd Ave
W 24th Ave
W King Edward Ave
W 26th Ave
W 27th Ave
W 28th Ave
W 29th Ave
Nanton Ave
Devonshire Cr
Connaught Dr
W 32nd Ave
W 33rd Ave
W 37th Ave
Granville St
Hudson St
Selkirk St
Osler St
Oak St
Laurel St
Willow St
Heather St
Cambie St
Yukon St
Talisman St
Columbia St
Manitoba St
Ontario St
Dinmont Ave
Peveril Ave
Midlothian Ave
Kersland Dr
Devonshire Park
Braemar Park
CAMBIE
BC Children's Hospital
King Edward
VanDusen Botanical Garden
Bloedel Conservatory 1
2
Queen Elizabeth Park
Hillcrest Park
15 Nat Bailey Stadium

Sights

Bloedel Conservatory GARDENS

1 MAP P119, E7

Cresting the hill in Queen Elizabeth Park, this domed conservatory is a delightful rainy-day warm-up. At Vancouver's best-value paid attraction, you'll find tropical trees and plants bristling with hundreds of free-flying, bright-plumaged birds. Listen for the noisy resident parrots but also keep your eyes peeled for the rainbow-hued Gouldian finches, shimmering African superb starlings and maybe even a dramatic Lady Amherst pheasant, snaking through the undergrowth.

Ask nicely and the attendants might let you feed the smaller birds from a bowl. (vandusengarden.org;)

Queen Elizabeth Park PARK

2 MAP P119, E7

The city's highest point – 167m above sea level and with panoramic views over the mountain-framed downtown skyscrapers – this 52-hectare park claims to house specimens of every tree native to Canada. Sports fields, manicured lawns and formal gardens keep the locals happy, and you'll likely also see wide-eyed couples posing for their wedding photos in particularly picturesque spots.

This is a good place to view local birdlife: you may spot chickadees, hummingbirds and huge bald eagles whirling high overhead. (vancouverparks.ca)

City Hall HISTORIC BUILDING

3 MAP P118, E2

Architecture fans should save time for one of Vancouver's best art-deco buildings. Completed in 1936, its highlights include a soaring, Gotham-style exterior as well as an interior of streamlined signs, cylindrical lanterns and embossed elevator doors.

Snap some photos of the statue of Captain George Vancouver outside, then check out the hand-

Behind the Deco Facade

The Great Depression caused major belt-tightening among regular folks in 1930s Vancouver. But despite the economic malaise, mayor Gerry McGeer spared no expense to build a new City Hall in 1936. Defended as a make-work project for the idled construction industry, the $1 million project (a huge sum for the time) was completed in just 12 months. Despite the controversy, the building is now one of Vancouver's most revered art-deco edifices.

If you're on a deco roll after admiring City Hall's architectural splendor, make sure you also hit downtown's magical Marine Building (p50).

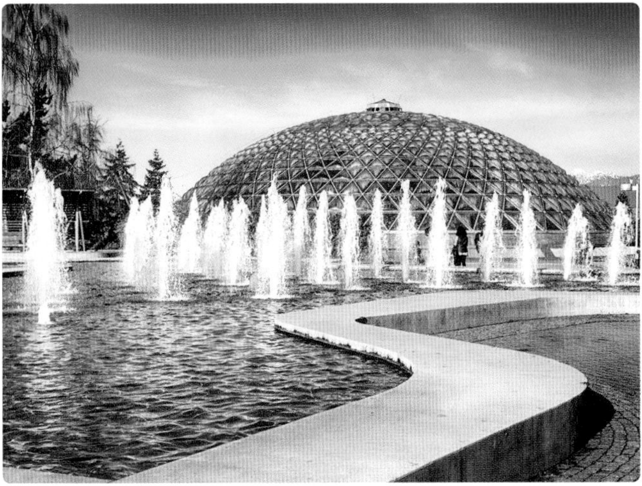
MR NIKON/SHUTTERSTOCK ©

Bloedel Conservatory, Queen Elizabeth Park

some wooden heritage mansions on surrounding Yukon St and W 12th Ave. Finally, snag a table at the public plaza next to City Hall for some grand mountain-framed cityscape views. (vancouver.ca)

Eating

Paul's Omelettery BREAKFAST $

4 MAP P118, A1

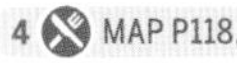

You'll be jostling for space with chatty locals at this breakfast and lunch joint near the south side of Granville Bridge. But it's worth it: the cozy, super-friendly place is superior to most bacon-and-eggs destinations. The menu is grounded in signature omelets while also offering excellent eggs Benedict and heaping 'lumberjack breakfasts.' Reservations are not accepted; arrive early on weekends. (paulsomelettery.com)

La Taquería Pinche Taco Shop MEXICAN $

5 MAP P118, E2

The latest finger-licking edition of this wildly popular Mexican mini-chain combines communal tables, a large patio and an inviting bar area with a full menu of favorites. Order a selection of meat and/or veggie tacos for the table (*al pastor* and *asada* recommended) and add some beers from Vancouver-based South American brewery Andina. Ask about afternoon and late-night happy-hour specials. (lataqueria.com)

Salmon n' Bannock

NORTHWESTERN US $$

6 MAP P118, B2

Vancouver's only Indigenous restaurant is an utterly delightful art-lined little bistro on an unassuming strip of Broadway shops. It's worth the easy bus trip, though, for fresh-made Indigenous-influenced dishes featuring local ingredients.

The juicy salmon 'n' bannock burger has been a staple here for years, but more elaborate, feast-like options include game sausages and bison pot roast. (salmonandbannock.net)

Tojo's

JAPANESE $$$

7 MAP P118, C2

Credited as the first restaurant on Vancouver's now vibrant sushi scene, this upscale, internationally recognized restaurant is more than a meal – it's an experience. Chef Tojo's *omakase* (personalized, chef-curated) menu is worth the splurge, drawing celebrity diners from around the world for a taste of the best Japanese food in the city. (tojos.com)

Christmas in Vancouver

From mid-November onwards, dozens of Yuletide offerings pop up around the city, from seasonal markets to festive stage shows to a giant annual parade.

One of the best places to tap into the Christmas spirit is VanDusen Botanical Garden (p114), which transforms into a colorful winter wonderland of fairy lights and spark-ling dioramas. Considering a festive city visit? See what else is on at vancouver christmasguide.com.

Heirloom Vegetarian

VEGETARIAN $$

8 MAP P118, A2

With a white-walled cafeteria-meets-rustic-artisan look, this is one of Vancouver's best vegetarian eateries, serving mostly BC and organic seasonal ingredients fused with international influences.

At dinner, the bulging felafel burger and cashew coconut curry are winners, but the all-day brunch has risen to prominence in recent years, especially the utterly delicious avocado eggs Benny. (heirloomveg.ca)

Vij's

INDIAN $$$

9 MAP P118, E3

Spicy aromas scent the air as you enter this warmly intimate dining space for Vancouver's finest Indian cuisine. Exemplary servers happily answer menu questions while bringing over snacks and chai.

There's a one-page array of tempting dishes, but the trick is to order three or four to share (mains are all available as small plates, and orders come with rice and naan). (vijs.ca; )

Summertime Ballgames

Catching a Vancouver Canadians (p125) minor-league baseball game at old-school **Nat Bailey Stadium** is a summer tradition for many locals. But for some the experience isn't complete unless you add a hot dog and some ice-cold beers to the proceedings. Enhancing the festivities are the non-baseball shenanigans, ranging from kiss cams to mascot races. Arguably the most fun you can have at a Vancouver spectator sport, it's also one of the most budget-friendly options (depending on how many hot dogs you put away).

Mazahr Lebanese Kitchen — LEBANESE $$

10 MAP P118, A2

Opened by former partner of Jamjar restaurant (p138), Mazahr provides the city with a taste of Lebanon, offering dishes that remind the chef of home. (mazahr.ca)

Drinking

Grapes & Soda — WINE BAR

11 MAP P118, A1

A warm, small-table hangout, Grapes & Soda self-identifies as a 'natural wine bar,' with well-curated options from BC, Europe and beyond.

This local favorite also serves excellent cocktails: from the countless bottles behind the bar, the staff can seemingly concoct anything your taste buds desire, whether or not it's on the menu. Need help? Slide into a Scotch, ginger and walnut Cortejo. (grapesandsoda.ca)

Small Victory — CAFE $

12 MAP P118, A3

The South Granville branch of this three-outlet local coffee chain serves up a sophisticated coffee program. If you're lucky enough to find one, snag a seat at the swanky white-and-gold bar and sip a silky-smooth latte served in a custom cup. If you're feeling snacky, add a flaky butter croissant to your order. (smallvictory.ca)

Caffe Barney — PUB

13 MAP P118, A3

Known as the 'barnyard' by locals, this upbeat *caffe* is a bustling brunch spot with a full bar (lunch and dinner menus are available as well). Choose a pint of local craft beer from the dozen varieties on tap, or go for a cocktail. If you can swing it, stop in for happy hour (3pm to 6pm, and 9pm to close every day). (caffebarney.com)

Animal Watch in the Neighborhoods

Common Critters

Vancouver's urban green spaces are home to a surprising array of creatures. Many of them roam the city's streets after dark, foraging for extra food.

During your visit, you'll find **black squirrels** everywhere, but don't be surprised to also spot **raccoons**. Common in several parks, they are often bold enough to hang out on porches and root through garbage bins. **Skunks** are almost as common, but the only time you'll likely see them is after an unfortunate roadkill incident (a fairly common occurrence around area parks). But while squirrels, raccoons and skunks are regarded as urban nuisances, some animals in the city are much larger.

Bigger Critters

Every spring, several Vancouver neighborhoods post notices of **coyote** spottings (there are an estimated 3000 living in and around the city). This is the time of year when these wild dogs build dens and raise pups, often in remote corners of city parks – and they become more protective of their territory in the process. This can lead to problems with domesticated pets. Vancouverites are warned to keep pets inside when coyotes are spotted in their neighborhoods, and to report any sightings to authorities.

Many locals will tell you they've only seen a coyote once or twice; these animals are adept at avoiding humans.

Animal Encounters

Human–animal interactions are an even bigger problem for areas that back directly onto wilderness regions. The North Shore is shadowed by a forest and mountain swathe that's long been a traditional home for **bears** – mostly black bears.

Residents in North Vancouver and West Vancouver know how to secure their garbage so as not to encourage bears to become habituated to human food. But every year – often in spring, when the hungry fur-balls are waking from hibernation – a few are trapped and relocated from the area.

For more information on wildlife (and guided nature walks) in the city, go to stanleyparkecology.ca.

Entertainment

Stanley Theatre

THEATER

14 MAP P118, A2

Popular musicals dominate early summer (usually the last show of the season) at this heritage theater, but the rest of the year sees new works and adaptations of contemporary hits from around the world.

Officially called the Stanley Industrial Alliance Stage (a moniker that not a single Vancouverite uses), the Stanley is part of the Arts Club Theatre Company, Vancouver's biggest. (artsclub.com)

Vancouver Canadians

BASEBALL

15 MAP P119, F7

Minor-league affiliates of the Toronto Blue Jays, the Canadians play at the charmingly old-school Nat Bailey Stadium. It's known as 'the prettiest ballpark in the world' thanks to its mountain backdrop. Afternoon games – called 'nooners' – are perfect for a nostalgic bask in the sun. Hot dogs and beer rule the menu, but there's also sushi and fruit – this is Vancouver, after all. (milb.com;)

Coyote

Vancouver Canadians, Nat Bailey Stadium (p125)

Shopping

Pacific Arts Market

ARTS & CRAFTS

16 MAP P118, A2

Head upstairs to this large, under-the-radar gallery space and you'll find a kaleidoscopic array of stands showcasing the work of more than 40 Vancouver and BC artists. From paintings to jewelry and from fiber arts to handmade chocolate bars, the wares on offer make authentic souvenirs to take back home. The artists change regularly and there's something for every budget. (pacificartsmarket.ca)

Walrus

HOMEWARES

17 MAP P118, E4

Small but brilliantly curated, Walrus teems with must-have accessories and home wares, mostly from Canadian designers.

Form meets function with everything on the shelves here, so give yourself plenty of time to browse the perfect pottery knickknacks, quirky artisan jewelry and raft of irresistible bags from Vancouver favorite Herschel Supply Co. Your credit card will soon be sweating. (walrushome.com)

Bacci's

HOMEWARES, CLOTHING

18 MAP P118, A2

Combining designer women's clothing on one side with a room full of perfectly curated trinkets piled high on antique wooden tables on the other, Bacci's is a dangerous place to browse. Before you know it, you'll have an armful of chunky luxury soaps, embroidered cushions and picture-perfect coffee mugs to fit in your suitcase. (baccis.ca)

Purdys Chocolates

CHOCOLATE

19 MAP P118, A2

Like a sweet beacon to the weary, this purple-painted chocolate purveyor stands at the corner of Granville St and W 11th Ave. It's a homegrown BC business with outlets dotted like candy sprinkles across the city, and it's hard not to pick up a few treats: go for chocolate hedgehogs, orange meltie bars or sweet Georgia browns (pecans in caramel and chocolate). (purdys.com)

Meinhardt Fine Foods

FOOD

20 MAP P118, A3

The culinary equivalent of a sex shop for food fans, this swanky deli and grocery emporium's narrow aisles are lined with international condiments, luxury canned goods and the kind of tempting treats that everyone should try at least once. Build a perfect picnic from the tempting bread, cheese and cold cuts, or snag one of the house-made deli sandwiches (paprika chicken recommended). (meinhardtfinefoods.com)

Explore

Kitsilano & University of British Columbia

Occupying the forest-fringed peninsula south of downtown, Vancouver's West Side includes two highlight neighborhoods: Kitsilano, with its large beaches, wood-built heritage homes and browsable 4th Ave shopping and dining district, and the University of British Columbia (UBC), a verdant campus with enough museums, attractions and dining options for a great alternative day out from the city center.

The Short List

- ***Nitobe Memorial Garden (p137)*** *Trekking through a tree-lined, traditional Japanese garden.*
- ***Museum of Vancouver (p136)*** *Noodling around nostalgic displays that illuminate the city of yesteryear.*
- ***Kitsilano Beach (p136)*** *Sunning yourself on the area's best beach before catching a free Kitsilano Showboat performance.*

Getting There & Around

Services 4 and 9 run through Kitsilano to UBC. The 99B-Line express bus runs along Broadway to UBC.

Take a Canada Line SkyTrain from downtown to Broadway-City Hall, then board the 99B-Line to UBC.

There is metered parking on and around W 4th and Broadway in Kitsilano. UBC has parkades and metered parking.

Kitsilano & University of British Columbia Map on p134

Nitobe Memorial Garden (p137) BOB POOL/SHUTTERSTOCK ©

Top Experience

See the Forest of Totem Poles at the Museum of Anthropology

MAP P134, C4

moa.ubc.ca

Vancouver's best museum is the main reason many visitors come to the University of British Columbia campus. The MOA is home to one of Canada's finest and most important collections of Northwest Coast Aboriginal art and artifacts. But the ambitious collection here goes way beyond local anthropological treasures, illuminating diverse cultures from around the world.

MOA 101

The highlight of the Arthur Erickson–designed museum, the **Great Hall** is a forest of towering totem poles plus a menagerie of carved ceremonial figures, house posts and delicate exhibits – all set against a giant floor-to-ceiling window facing the waterfront and mountains. Many carvings are surprisingly vibrantly colored: look out for smiling masks plus a life-size rowing boat containing two figures that look ready to head straight out to sea. The Great Hall is also where the museum's **free tours** start several times a day: these provide an excellent overview of what else there is to see here.

At the time of going to print, MOA was closed for seismic updates of the Great Hall. It was due to re-open early this year, so some things may have changed since our last visit. We recommend to check the website to see if it is open and book your visit.

Getting Lost

This is also a great museum to lose yourself in. The **Gallery of Northwest Coast Master works** combines breathtaking smaller creations, such as intricate ceremonial headdresses, with the recorded voices of Aboriginal artisans contextualizing the exhibits. Nearby, the jam-packed **Multiversity Galleries** teem with 10,000 ethnographic artifacts from around the world, with everything from Kenyan snuff bottles to Swedish lace doilies. Save time for the **European Ceramics Gallery**, a subtle stunner lined with pottery and porcelain made between the 16th and 19th centuries.

Value-Added Extras

Diverse temporary exhibitions are staged here throughout the year. Check MOA's website for upcoming openings. Also, discover the site's **Outdoor Exhibits** area, with its Haida houses and Musqueam house posts.

★ Top Tips.

- There are free tours, included with entry, on most days. Check at the front desk for times.
- Entry to the Outdoor Exhibits area is free and does not require a ticket.
- There are several other attractions on campus; ask at the front desk for combined ticket options that include entry to some of these other UBC sites.

Take a Break

The MOA is a short walk from the excellent Koerner's Pub, where you can drink and dine with the students.

Time your visit well and you can also pick up a few treats at one of the **UBC Farm Markets** (ubcfarm.ubc.ca/food).

Walking Tour

UBC Campus & Gardens Walk

The region's biggest university campus has plenty of attractions for a full day out. But while transit makes UBC easy to reach from downtown, you'll feel like you've traveled far from the city. This walk leads you to some of the university's biggest and also lesser-known attractions. Keep your eyes peeled en route for the many public artworks that dot the campus.

Walk Facts

Start Morris & Helen Belkin Art Gallery

End UBC Botanical Garden

Length 3km; 1½ hours

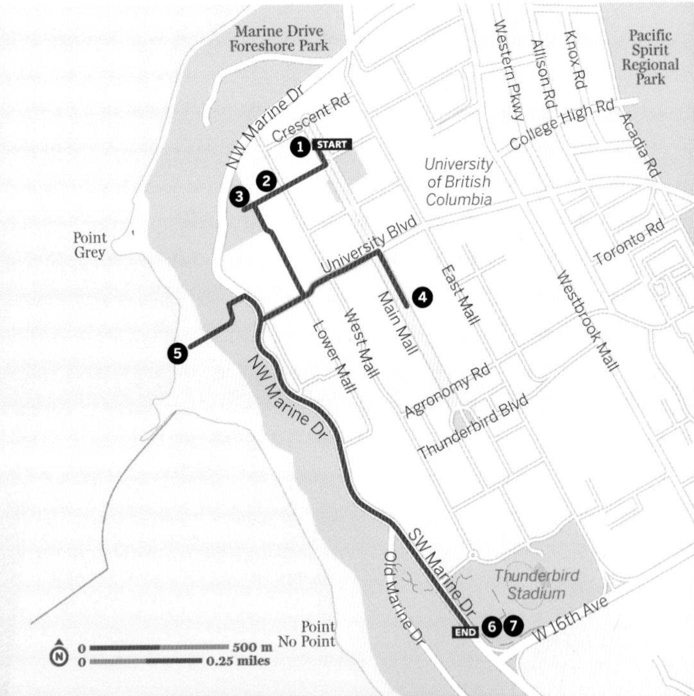

❶ Morris & Helen Belkin Art Gallery

One of Vancouver's oldest contemporary art spaces, the Morris & Helen Belkin Art Gallery (p138) stages changing (and sometimes quite provocative) exhibitions that are always worth checking out. Consult the website for info on openings.

❷ UBC Asian Centre

The campus is studded with landscaped gardens and green spaces, but the one outside the UBC Asian Centre is arguably the most unusual. Check out the hulking rock garden boulders here, each inscribed with Confucian philosophies.

❸ Nitobe Memorial Garden

Just a few steps away, the utterly delightful Nitobe Memorial Garden (p137) is an oasis of traditional Japanese horticultural tranquility. Look for turtles basking on the pond's grass-banked shoreline and check ahead for summertime tours that explain some of the garden's symbolic features.

❹ Beaty Biodiversity Museum

Head into Vancouver's Beaty Biodiversity Museum (p136) and discover the variety of flora and fauna found in the area – and beyond. Be sure to take in the blue-whale skeleton on display: the Beaty is one of the few places in the world where you can get an up-close look at the remains of the largest creature ever to have existed on Earth.

❺ Wreck Beach

If you're feeling adventurous, look for the signs for Trail 6, walk between the trees and descend to Wreck Beach (p138). Vancouver's official naturist beach, it provides the perfect opportunity to drop your drawers with a few like-minded locals.

❻ UBC Botanical Garden

Make sure you put your pants back on before reaching the final attraction. UBC Botanical Garden (p137) is a verdant green space that's divided into a dense forest swathe on one side and several themed horticultural areas on the other.

❼ Greenheart TreeWalk

If you're visiting from April to October, try to fit in a stroll along the Greenheart TreeWalk (p137) before you leave the UBC Botanical Garden. The aerial trail system takes you from tree to tree through coastal temperate rainforest, providing a squirrel's-eye view of the forest floor below.

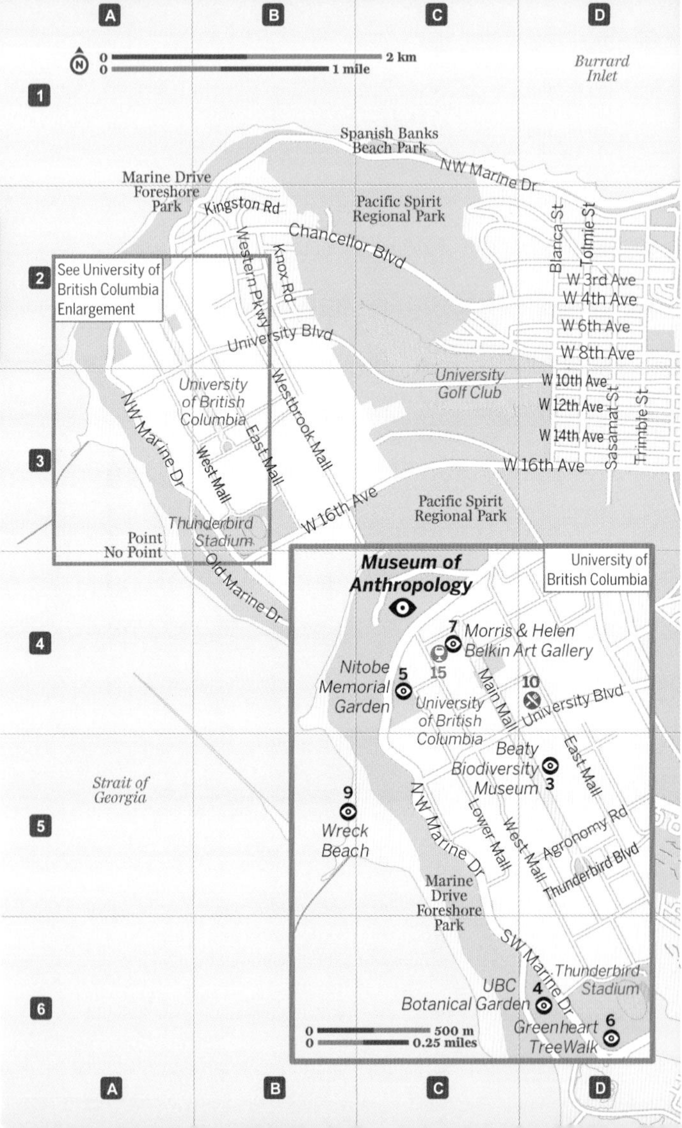

A B C D

0 2 km
0 1 mile

Burrard Inlet
Spanish Banks Beach Park
NW Marine Dr
Marine Drive Foreshore Park
Kingston Rd
Pacific Spirit Regional Park
Chancellor Blvd
Blanca St
Tolmie St
W 3rd Ave
W 4th Ave
W 6th Ave
W 8th Ave
W 10th Ave
W 12th Ave
W 14th Ave
W 16th Ave
Sasamat St
Trimble St
University Golf Club
See University of British Columbia Enlargement
Western Pkwy
Knox Rd
University Blvd
University of British Columbia
Westbrook Mall
East Mall
West Mall
NW Marine Dr
Thunderbird Stadium
Point No Point
W 16th Ave
Pacific Spirit Regional Park
Old Marine Dr
Strait of Georgia

University of British Columbia
Museum of Anthropology
7 Morris & Helen Belkin Art Gallery
15
5 Nitobe Memorial Garden
10
University Blvd
Main Mall
University of British Columbia
Beaty Biodiversity Museum 3
East Mall
9 Wreck Beach
NW Marine Dr
Lower Mall
West Mall
Agronomy Rd
Thunderbird Blvd
Marine Drive Foreshore Park
SW Marine Dr
Thunderbird Stadium
UBC Botanical Garden 4
Greenheart TreeWalk 6
0 500 m
0 0.25 miles

1 2 3 4 5 6

E
F
G
H
For reviews see
Top Experiences p130
Sights p136
Eating p138
Drinking p140
Entertainment p141
Shopping p141
English Bay
Beach Ave
1
See Kitsilano Enlargement
Vanier Park
Jericho Beach
Jericho Beach Park
W 1st Ave
Point Grey Rd
Cornwall Ave
2
W 3rd Ave
12 11
Larch St
Balsam St
W 2nd Ave
W 4th Ave
Burrard St
Department of National Defence
Alma St
W 7th Ave
Bayswater St
KITSILANO
W 6th Ave
W 8th Ave
Granville St
W Broadway
W Broadway
POINT GREY
Crown St
Wallace St
Highbury St
Collingwood St
Blenheim St
Balaclava St
Macdonald St
Connaught Park
Arbutus St
W 13th Ave
Fir St
3
W 15th Ave
W 16th Ave
W 18th Ave
Carnarvon Park
W 20th Ave
W 20th Ave
Yew St
Cypress St
Kitsilano
Vancouver Maritime Museum
8
English Bay
18
1
W King Edward Ave
4
Museum of Vancouver
Whyte Ave
Chestnut St
Kitsilano Beach
2
Creelman Ave
Vanier Park
Burrard St
Kitsilano Beach Park
17
W 33rd Ave
Cornwall Ave
York Ave
Larch St
Balsam St
Vine St
W 1st Ave
W 2nd Ave
Maple St
Cypress St
Burrard St
Fir St
5
19
W 3rd Ave
14
W 4th Ave
16
22
Arbutus Greenway
W 5th Ave
13
Granville St
Trafalgar St
W 6th Ave
Yew St
Arbutus St
W 7th Ave
W 7th Ave
W 8th Ave
W 8th Ave
21
Larch St
W Broadway
Maple St
Pine St
Fir St
W 10th Ave
6
Connaught Park
20
KITSILANO
0 500 m
0 0.25 miles
W 12th Ave
E
F
G
H

Sights

Museum of Vancouver MUSEUM

1 MAP P135, G4

The MOV serves up cool temporary exhibitions alongside in-depth permanent galleries of fascinating First Nations artifacts and evocative pioneer-era exhibits. But it really comes to life in its vibrant 1950s pop culture and 1960s hippie counterculture sections, a reminder that Kitsilano was once the grass-smoking center of Vancouver's flower-power movement.

Look out for a new vintage-mahogany exhibit that showcases works by both emerging and seasoned local designers. (museumofvancouver.ca;)

Kitsilano Beach BEACH

2 MAP P135, F4

Facing English Bay, Kits Beach is one of Vancouver's favorite summertime hangouts. The wide, sandy expanse attracts buff Frisbee tossers, giggling volleyball players, and those who just like to preen while catching the rays. The ocean is fine for a dip, though serious swimmers should consider the heated **Kitsilano Pool** (vancouver parks.ca;), one of the world's largest outdoor saltwater pools.

Beaty Biodiversity Museum MUSEUM

3 MAP P134, D5

The family-friendly Beaty Biodiversity Museum showcases a two-million-item natural-history

Kitsilano Beach

CDRIN/SHUTTERSTOCK ©

collection including birds, fossils and herbarium displays. The highlight is the 25m blue-whale skeleton, artfully displayed in the two-story entranceway. Don't miss the first display case, crammed with a beady-eyed menagerie of tooth-and-claw taxidermy.

Consider visiting on the third Thursday of the month, when entry is by donation after 5pm and the museum stays open until 8:30pm; there's often a special theme or live performance for these monthly nocturnal events. (beatymuseum.ubc.ca)

UBC Botanical Garden GARDENS

4 ◉ MAP P134, D6

You'll find a huge array of rhododendrons, a fascinating apothecary plot, and a winter green space of cold-weather bloomers in this 28-hectare complex of themed gardens. Among the towering trees, look for northern flicker woodpeckers and chittering little Douglas squirrels.

Also save time for the attraction's Greenheart TreeWalk, which elevates visitors up to 23m above the forest floor on a 310m guided ecotour. The combined garden and Greenheart ticket costs adult/child $23/10. (botanicalgarden.ubc.ca; 👪)

Nitobe Memorial Garden GARDENS

5 ◉ MAP P134, C4

Exemplifying Japanese horticultural philosophies, this is a delightfully tranquil green oasis of peaceful pathways, small traditional bridges, and a large, moss-banked pond filled with plump koi. It's named after Dr Inazo Nitobe, a scholar whose mug appears on Japan's ¥5000 bill.

Consider a springtime visit for the florid cherry-blossom displays and keep an eye out for the occasional turtle basking in the sun. (botanicalgarden.ubc.ca/nitobe)

HR MacMillan Space Centre MUSEUM

Focusing on the wonderful world of space, this kid-favorite museum (see 1 ◉ Map p135, G4) includes a gallery of hands-on exhibits (don't miss the Mars section, where you can drive across the surface in a simulator) as well as a menu of live science demonstrations in the small theater and a cool 45-minute planetarium show upstairs. Check the daily schedule of shows and presentations online before you arrive. The Saturday-night planetarium performances are popular with locals and typically draw a more adult crowd. (spacecentre.ca)

Greenheart TreeWalk AMUSEMENT PARK

6 ◉ MAP P134, D6

One of the best ways to commune with nature is to pretend you're a squirrel. While costumes are not required for this cool canopy walkway (you may win a raised eyebrow if you chance it), visitors love swaying across the steel bridges and noodling around the wooden platforms up to 23m from the forest floor. It's inside UBC Botanical Garden (p137). Greenheart admission includes entry to the TreeWalk. (botanicalgarden.ubc.ca;)

Morris & Helen Belkin Art Gallery

GALLERY

7 MAP P134, C4

This ever-intriguing gallery specializes in contemporary and often quite challenging pieces, with chin-stroking new exhibitions opening in its high-ceilinged, white-walled spaces throughout the year. Check ahead for workshops and presentations, often covering key or emerging themes in avant-garde art. (belkin.ubc.ca)

Vancouver Maritime Museum

MUSEUM

8 MAP P135, G4

Teeming with salty seafaring artifacts, dozens of intricate ship models and a couple of walk-through recreated boat sections, this waterfront A-frame museum is also home to the *St Roch*, a 1928 Royal Canadian Mounted Police Arctic patrol vessel that was the first to navigate the Northwest Passage in both directions.

Entry includes timed access to this celebrated boat, and you can also try your hand at piloting it via a cool wheelhouse simulator. (vancouvermaritimemuseum.com;)

Wreck Beach

BEACH

9 MAP P134, B5

Follow Trail 6 from UBC into the woods and down the steep steps to find Vancouver's only official naturist beach, complete with a motley crew of counterculture locals, independent vendors and sunburned regulars.

The pants-free bunch are a generally welcoming group, so long as you're not just there to gawk; start your visit on the right foot by quickly peeling off in solidarity. (wreckbeach.org)

Eating

Jamjar Canteen

LEBANESE $

10 MAP P134, D4

Visiting Canteen, a simplified version of the city's highly popular Jamjar Lebanese comfort-food restaurants, means choosing from four mains (lamb sausages or deep-fried cauliflower recommended), then adding the approach: rice bowl, salad bowl or wrap. Round out your meal by choosing from olives, veggies, hummus and more, then dive into your hearty lunch or dinner. (jamjarcanteen.ca;)

Naam

VEGETARIAN $

11 MAP P135, G2

An evocative relic of Kitsilano's hippie past, this vegetarian restaurant has the feel of a comfy farmhouse. It's not unusual to wait for a table at peak times, but it's worth it for the huge menu of hearty stir-fries, nightly curry specials, bulging quesadillas and ever-popular fries with miso gravy.

It's the kind of veggie spot where carnivores delightedly dine. (thenaam.com;)

Linh Cafe FRENCH, VIETNAMESE $$

12 MAP P135, F2

Arrive outside peak times at this chatty locals' favorite, a friendly, red-tabled restaurant serving French bistro classics and enticing Vietnamese specialties. You'll find everything from escargot to steak *frites* on the eclectic menu, but make a beeline for the deliciously brothy beef *pho*. On your way out, add a shiny little palmier pastry and a Vietnamese coffee to go. (linhcafe.com)

Fable Kitchen CANADIAN $$

13 MAP P135, F5

One of Vancouver's favorite farm-to-table restaurants is a lovely rustic-chic room of exposed brick, wood beams and prominently displayed red rooster logos. But looks are just part of the appeal. Expect perfectly prepared bistro dishes showcasing local seasonal ingredients such as duck, pork and scallops. It's great gourmet comfort food with little pretension, hence the packed room most nights. Reservations recommended. (fablekitchen.ca)

Maenam THAI $$

14 MAP P135, F5

Kitsilano's best Thai restaurant is a contemporary reinvention of the concept, with subtle, complex influences flavoring the menu in a warm, wood-floored room with an inviting ambience. You can start with the familiar (although even the pad Thai here is eye-poppingly different), but save room for something new, such as the utterly delicious lamb shank with red cumin curry. (maenam.ca;)

Ways to Save Your Cash

The **Vanier Park Explore Pass** costs $42.50/36.40 per adult/child and covers entry to the Museum of Vancouver (MOV), the Vancouver Maritime Museum and the HR MacMillan Space Centre. It's available at each of the three attractions and can save you around $10 on individual adult entry. There's also a **Dual Pass** (adult/child $31.50/18.50) that covers the MOV and Space Centre only.

You can also save with two separate passes at the university. The **UBC Museums Pass** (adult/child/family $25/20/60) includes entry to the Beaty Biodiversity Museum, while the **UBC Gardens and MOA Pass** (adult/child/family $27/23/65) covers the UBC Botanical Garden and Nitobe Memorial Garden.

Drinking

Koerner's Pub

PUB

15 MAP P134, C4

UBC's best pub welcomes with its communal tables, foliage-fringed patio, and clientele of nerdy professors and hipster regulars. There's an excellent booze list; dive into BC craft beers from the likes of Driftwood and Strange Fellows. Hungry? The Koerner organic burger is a staple, but also recommended is the crunchy UBC farm harvest salad, largely sourced from the university's own farm. (koerners.ca)

49th Parallel Coffee

COFFEE

16 MAP P135, F5

At Kitsilano's favorite coffee-shop hangout you can sit with locals in the glass-enclosed conservatory-like area (handy in deluge-prone Raincouver) and sip your latte from a turquoise cup. Be sure to scoff as many own-brand Luckys Doughnuts as you can manage; just because they're artisanal, that doesn't mean you should have only one. Need a recommendation? Try an apple-bacon fritter. Or two. (49thcoffee.com)

Bard on the Beach

Vancouver's Bold New Park

When the City of Vancouver splashed out $55 million on an 8.5km stretch of disused railway line running from Kitsilano to Marpole, some locals questioned the purchase. But the **Arbutus Greenway** (vancouver.ca/parks;) has since become popular with locals who love walking or cycling this wide, nature-hugging trail. Plans are still being finalized for the park's permanent features, but whatever happens this flora-flanked corridor is here to stay.

Corduroy — BAR

17 MAP P135, F4

Near the first bus stop after the Burrard Bridge (coming from downtown), this intimate, cave-like hangout is arguably Kitsilano's best late-night haunt. Slide onto a seat and peruse the beady-eyed taxidermy, then order a pitcher of house beer from the shingle-backed bar. A lively show roster (check ahead via the Facebook page) often includes bands, comedy or open-mic shenanigans. (corduroyrestaurant.com)

Entertainment

Bard on the Beach — PERFORMING ARTS

18 MAP P135, G4

Watching Shakespeare performed while the sun sets over the mountains beyond the tented main stage is a Vancouver summertime highlight. There are usually three Shakespeare plays, plus one Bard-related work (*Rosencrantz and Guildenstern are Dead*, for example), to choose from during the season. Q&A talks are staged after some Tuesday performances.

Opera, fireworks and wine-tasting nights are held throughout the season. (bardonthebeach.org;)

Khatsahlano Street Party — MUSIC

19 MAP P135, F5

If you're in Vancouver in July, be sure to add the Khatsahlano Street Party – Vancouver's largest free music and arts festival – to your calendar. A 10-block stretch of the bustling West 4th area sets the stage for top local performers and artisans, plus great food and a beer garden. (khatsahlano.com)

Shopping

Kitsilano Farmers Market — MARKET

20 MAP P135, E6

This seasonal farmers market is one of the city's most popular and is Kitsilano's best excuse to get out and hang with the locals. Arrive early for the best selection – you'll have the pick of freshly

The Dope on Local Pot Shops

Backstory

Just a few years ago, Vancouver had dozens of storefront marijuana dispensaries operating in a gray area of law that accepted the personal use of cannabis for medical reasons. Many locals and several of these stores made an art form out of proving this medical need. At the same time, the local police generally turned a blind eye.

Law Change

This pot smoke of confusion cleared in 2018 when the federal government legalized the recreational use of cannabis in Canada. The city and the province quickly moved to regulate this 'Wild West' industry. Rather than navigate the rigorous licensing laws that ensued, many weed stores that had popped up over the preceding few years suddenly shut down.

Pot Shops Go Legit

The 2.0 version of Vancouver's cannabis retail scene has now emerged, with licensed shops and mini-chains including **City Cannabis Co**, **Dutch Love Cannabis** and **Evergreen Cannabis** now serving curious customers around the city. And where do they get their grass? The province's BC Liquor Distribution Branch, long-time controller of booze sales in the region, is now the only legal way for private pot shops to source supplies for recreational resale.

It remains to be seen if this new business model will thrive or if long-time 'BC bud' users will keep buying from their friendly (and typically cheaper) neighborhood suppliers.

Need to Know

If you're curious about these stores, nip inside and chat to the staff about how it all works and what they can sell you. Keep in mind that, although recreational cannabis is now legal in Canada, you are not permitted to transport your purchases across international borders.

More info? Read up via the province's BC Cannabis Stores website: bccannabisstores.com.

plucked local fruit and veg, such as sweet strawberries or spectacularly flavorful heirloom tomatoes. You'll likely never want to shop in a mainstream supermarket again. (eatlocal.org)

Kidsbooks

BOOKS

21 MAP P135, E6

From *Dolphin Boy* to *The Wonky Donkey*, this huge, highly inviting store – reputedly Canada's biggest children's bookstore – has thousands of novels, picture books and anything else you can think of to keep your bookish young ones happy.

There are regular author events (check ahead via the website), plus quality toys and games to provide a break from all that strenuous page-turning. (kidsbooks.ca;)

Zulu Records

MUSIC

22 MAP P135, F5

Kitsilano's fave indie music store has downsized in recent years, but it's still easy to blow an afternoon here with the vinyl and CD nerds, flicking through the new, used and hard-to-find albums.

It also sells local show tickets, while the knowledgeable staffers can point you to any essential Vancouver recordings worth buying (ask for a copy of *Last Call*). (facebook.com/zulurecords.store)

Fashion Finds

Melanie Auld
(melanieauld.com)
The flagship Vancouver location of sought-after Canadian jewelry brand Melanie Auld has beautiful displays of demi-fine jewelry, along with a welded-bracelet station and a piercing room.

Poppy Barley
(poppybarley.com)
Certified B Corporation Poppy Barley creates luxury footwear at a fair price. Co-owned by sisters, the brand continues to rethink every step of how it creates its sustainable products, designed to be worn on repeat.

Old Faithful
(oldfaithfulshop.com)
Owner Walter Manning was inspired by his grandparents' shop. It's a modern-day version of a general provisions store, featuring quality products with beautiful design elements. Manning aspires for the products he sells to become known as 'old faithfuls': trusty, well-built heirloom pieces that are only enhanced by the passage of time.

Recommended by Lyndi Barrett, *fashion publicist and trend expert, @StyleCalling*

Survival Guide

Before You Go 146

Book Your Stay ... 146

When to Go ... 146

Arriving in Vancouver 147

Getting Around 148

Bus ... 148

SkyTrain ... 148

SeaBus ... 148

Miniferry ... 148

Bicycle ... 149

Car & Motorcycle ... 149

Taxi ... 149

Essential Information 150

Accessible Travel ... 150

Business Hours ... 150

Discount Cards ... 150

Electricity ... 151

Money ... 151

Public Holidays ... 152

Safe Travel ... 152

Telephone ... 152

Tourist Information ... 152

Visas ... 152

Responsible Travel ... 153

Vancouver International Airport (p147) ABERU.GO/SHUTTERSTOCK ©

Before You Go

Book Your Stay

- More than 25,000 hotel, B&B and hostel rooms available, the majority in or around the downtown core.
- Book far ahead for summer. Rates peak in July and August, but there are good spring and fall deals (alongside increased rainy days).
- Airbnb operates in Vancouver, although a regulatory crackdown has reduced their number in recent years.

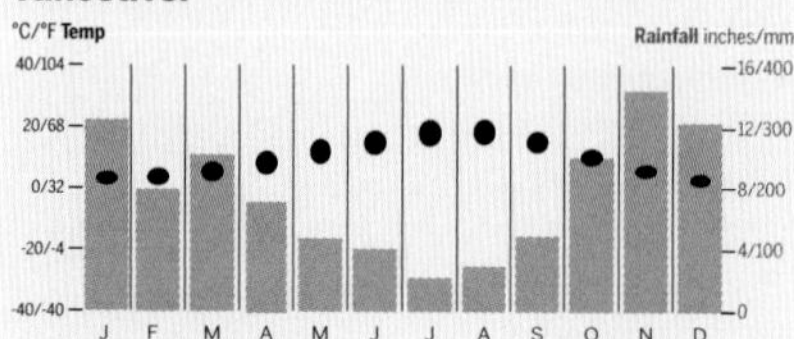

When to Go

- **Winter (Dec–Feb)** Chilly and damp but rarely massively snowy, except on local ski slopes. Some clear but crisp days included.
- **Spring (Mar–May)** Rain, some sun and good off-peak hotel rates. Great time to visit the sites and attractions.
- **Summer (Jun–Aug)** Vancouver's blue-skied peak. T-shirts recommended; expect to find crowded visitor attractions.
- **Fall (Sep–Nov)** Rain returns but still plenty of golden sunny days as the leaves descend. Another good time for hotel deals.

Useful Websites

- **Tourism Vancouver** (tourismvancouver.com) Wide range of accommodations listings and package deals.
- **Hello BC** (hellobc.com) Official Destination British Columbia (BC) accommodations search engine.
- **Accredited BC Accommodations Association** (accreditedaccommodations.ca) Wide range of B&Bs in Vancouver and around the province.
- **Lonely Planet** (lonelyplanet.com/canada/vancouver/hotels) Recommendations and bookings.

Best Budget

- **YWCA Hotel** (ywcahotel.com) Centrally located with comfortable rooms that offer great value (especially for families).
- **HI Vancouver Downtown** (hihostels.ca) Actually located in the West End; a quieter hostel with good family rooms.
- **Samesun Backpackers Lodge** (samesun.com) Right on downtown's Granville Strip entertainment district; perfect for partyers.
- **HI Vancouver Central** (hihostels.ca) Centrally located hostel with lots of small rooms.

Best Midrange

- **Victorian Hotel** (victorianhotel.ca) Steps from Gastown; mix of large and Euro-style smaller rooms.
- **The Sunset** (sunsetinn.com) West End hotel with large, kitchen-equipped rooms.
- **Sylvia Hotel** (sylviahotel.com) Ivy-covered heritage hotel with some waterfront-view rooms.
- **Skwachàys Lodge** (skwachays.com) Boutique Aboriginal arts hotel and gallery, the first of its kind in Canada.

Best Top End

- **Fairmont Pacific Rim** (fairmont.com) Chic downtown property steps from the waterfront.
- **The DOUGLAS, Autograph Collection** (marriott.com) Sustainable design with boutique feel, center of the city's entertainment district.
- **Rosewood Hotel Georgia** (rosewoodhotels.com) Stylish sleepover for those who like to see and be seen.
- **Wedgewood Hotel & Spa** (wedgewoodhotel.com) This classic deluxe hotel is dripping with elegant flourishes.

Arriving in Vancouver

Vancouver International Airport

- Located 13km south of Vancouver in the city of Richmond, **YVR** (yvr.ca) has two main terminals and receives flights from BC, North America and around the world.
- **TransLink** Canada Line SkyTrain services run from the airport to Vancouver, taking around 25 minutes to reach downtown and costing from $8 to $10.90.
- **Taxi** Fares to downtown Vancouver are around $35.
- **Ride share** There are three pickup locations around the airport.
- **Hire car** Desks are located inside the airport.

Pacific Central Station

- Pacific Central Station is the city's main terminus for long-distance trains from across Canada on VIA Rail (viarail.com), and from Seattle (just south of the border) and beyond on Amtrak (amtrak.com).
- Intercity bus services also roll in here, including **Greyhound** (greyhound.com) services from Seattle, and **BC Connector** (bcconnector.com) services from Kelowna, Kamloops, Whistler and Victoria.
- The Main St-Science World SkyTrain station is just across the street for connections to downtown and beyond.
- There are car-rental desks in the station, and cabs and ride-share services are also available just outside the building.

BC Ferries

- **BC Ferries** (bcferries.com) services arrive at Tsawwassen, an hour south of Vancouver, and at Horseshoe Bay, 30 minutes from downtown in West Vancouver. These services arrive from points around BC, including Victoria.

- To reach downtown from Tsawwassen via transit, take bus 620 (adult/child $5.90/4.05) to Bridgeport Station in Richmond and transfer to the Canada Line. It takes about an hour to reach the city center.
- From Horseshoe Bay to downtown, take bus 257 (adult/child $4.35/3). It takes about 40 minutes.

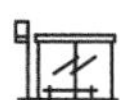

Getting Around

Bus

- Vancouver's **TransLink** (translink.ca) bus network is extensive. All vehicles have bike racks and all are wheelchair accessible.
- Exact change (or more) is required; buses use fare machines and change is not given. Tickets are valid for up to 90 minutes of transfer travel. While Vancouver's transit system covers three geographic fare zones, all bus trips are regarded as one-zone fares.
- Bus services operate from early morning to after midnight in central areas. There is also a 12-route NightBus system that runs from 2am. Look out for the NightBus signs at designated stops.

SkyTrain

- TransLink's SkyTrain rapid-transit network is a great way to move around the region, especially beyond the city center.
- Compass tickets for SkyTrain trips can be purchased from station vending machines (change is given; machines also accept debit and credit cards) prior to boarding.
- SkyTrain's Canada Line links the city to Richmond and the airport.
- The Expo Line operates services from downtown to the cities of Surrey and Burnaby.
- The Millennium Line links Vancouver's VCC-Clark Station to the cities of Burnaby, Coquitlam and Port Moody.

SeaBus

- The iconic SeaBus public-transit water shuttle (regular transit fares apply) takes 15 minutes to cross Burrard Inlet between Waterfront Station and North Vancouver's Lonsdale Quay.
- At Lonsdale you can then connect to buses servicing North Vancouver and West Vancouver, including the 236 to both Capilano Suspension Bridge and Grouse Mountain.
- SeaBus services leave from Waterfront Station between 6:16am and 1:22am, Monday to Saturday (8:16am to 11:16pm on Sunday).
- Tickets must be purchased from vending machines on either side of the route before boarding.

Miniferry

- There are two private miniferry operators in the city. Single trips on either operator cost from $3.50.
- **Aquabus Ferries** (theaquabus.com) Runs between the foot of Hornby St and Granville Island. It also services

several additional spots along the False Creek waterfront, as far as Science World.

- **False Creek Ferries** (granvilleislandferries.bc.ca) Operates a similar Granville Island service from Sunset Beach, and has additional ports of call around False Creek.

Bicycle

- Vancouver is a good cycling city, with 300km of designated neighborhood and downtown routes.
- You can take your bike for free on SkyTrain, SeaBus and regular bus transit services.
- Cyclists are required by law to wear helmets.
- Locals and visitors can use **Mobi** (mobibikes.ca), a public bike-share scheme.
- Download free cycle-route maps from the TransLink website (translink.ca) or plan your route using vancouver.bikerouteplanner.com.

Car & Motorcycle

- For most Vancouver sightseeing, you'll be fine without a car.

Transit Tickets & Passes

- Along with trip-planning resources, the TransLink website (translink.ca) has a comprehensive section on fares and passes covering its combined bus, SeaBus and SkyTrain services.
- The transit system is divided into three geographic zones. One-zone trips cost adult/child $3.05/2, two zones $4.35/3 and three zones $5.90/4.05. All bus trips are one-zone fares. If you buy a stored-value Compass Card, fares are charged at a lower rate.
- You can buy single-use tickets and all-access DayPasses (adult/child $10.75/8.45) from vending machines at SeaBus and SkyTrain stations. You can also buy stored-value Compass Cards ($6 deposit) from these machines or at designated Compass retailers around the city, including London Drugs branches.
- After 6:30pm, and on weekends or holidays, all transit trips are classed as one-zone fares. Children 12 and under ride free.

- For visits incorporating the wider region's mountains and communities, a vehicle makes life much simpler: the further you travel from downtown, the more limited your transit options become.
- Parking is at a premium in downtown Vancouver. There are some free spots on residential side streets, but many require permits, and traffic wardens are predictably predatory. For an interactive map of parking-lot locations, see EasyPark (easypark.ca).

Taxi

Vancouver has rideshare services including Uber and Lyft, or try the following long-established taxi companies:

Black Top & Checker Cabs (btccabs.ca)

Vancouver Taxi (vancouvertaxi.cab)

Yellow Cab (yellowcabonline.com)

Essential Information

Accessible Travel

- On your arrival at the airport, vehicle-rental agencies can provide prearranged cars with hand controls. Accessible cabs are also widely available at the airport and throughout the city, on request.
- All TransLink SkyTrain, SeaBus and transit bus services are wheelchair accessible. Check the TransLink website (translink.ca) for a wide range of information on accessible transport around the region. Head to travel.gc.ca/travelling/health-safety/disabilities for information and resources on accessible travel across Canada. In addition, download Lonely Planet's free Accessible Travel guides from shop.lonelyplanet.com/en-ca/products/accessible-travel-online-resources.
- Service dogs may legally be brought into restaurants, hotels and other businesses in Vancouver.
- Almost all downtown sidewalks have sloping ramps. Most public buildings and attractions are wheelchair accessible.
- Check the City of Vancouver's dedicated website (vancouver.ca/accessibility) for information and resources.
- **Disability Alliance BC** (disabilityalliancebc.org) provides programs and support for people with disabilities.
- **CNIB** (cnib.ca) has support and services for the visually impaired.
- **Western Institute for the Deaf & Hard of Hearing** (wavefrontcentre.ca) has interpreter services and resources for the hearing impaired. Its operating name is the Wavefront Centre for Communication Accessibility.

Business Hours

Most business hours are consistent throughout the year, with the exception of attractions, which often reduce their hours slightly outside the summer.

Banks 9am to 5pm weekdays, with some opening Saturday mornings.

Shops 10am to 6pm Monday to Saturday; noon to 5pm Sunday.

Restaurants 11:30am to 3pm and 5pm to 10pm.

Coffee shops and cafes From 8am, some earlier.

Pubs and bars Pubs open from 11:30am; bars often open from 5pm. They close at midnight or later.

Discount Cards

- **Vancouver City Passport** (citypassports.com; $39.99) Discounts at attractions, restaurants and activities across the city for up to two adults and two children.
- **Museums Pass** (vancouverattractions.com/museums-pass) Choose from 10 museums and galleries, and receive savings when you book two or more.
- **UBC Gardens & MOA Pass** (adult/child/family $27/23/65) Combined entry to the Museum of Anthropology (MOA), UBC Botanical Garden and Nitobe Memorial Garden, plus 10% discount in their gift shops.

- **Vancouver Attractions Group** (vancouverattractions.com) Coupons and discounted entry tickets are available for multiple Vancouver-area attractions.

Electricity

Type A
120V/60Hz

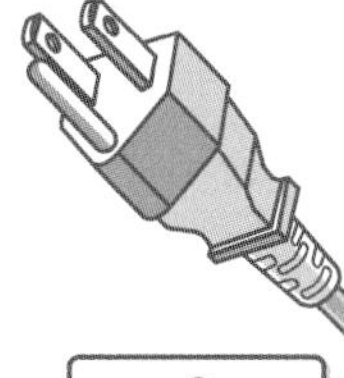

Type B
120V/60Hz

Money

ATMs are available all around the city. Credit cards are widely accepted and used at all accommodations and almost all shops and restaurants.

Credit Cards

- Visa, MasterCard and American Express are widely accepted in Canada.
- Credit cards can get you cash advances at bank ATMs, usually for an additional surcharge.
- Be aware that many US-based credit cards often convert foreign charges using unfavorable exchange rates and fees.

Changing Money

- You can exchange currency at most main bank branches, which often charge less than the *bureaux de change* dotted around the city.
- In addition to the banks, try **Vancouver Bullion & Currency Exchange** (vbce.ca), which often offers a wider range of currencies and competitive rates.

ATMs

- Interbank ATM exchange rates usually beat the rates offered for traveler's checks or foreign currency.
- Canadian ATM fees are generally low, but it is possible that your home bank may charge another fee on top of that.
- Some ATMs also dispense US currency, which is ideal if you're planning a trip across the border.
- ATMs abound in Vancouver, with bank branches congregating around the business district bordered by Burrard, Georgia, Pender and Granville Sts. You will find that drugstores also frequently have ATMs.

Tipping

- **Restaurant waitstaff** 15% to 18%
- **Bar servers** $1 per drink
- **Hotel bellhops** $2 per bag
- **Taxis** 10% to 15%

Public Holidays

During national public holidays, banks, schools and government offices (including post offices) are closed, and transportation, museums and other services often operate on Sunday schedules. Holidays falling on weekends are usually observed the following Monday.

Major public holidays in Vancouver:

- **New Year's Day** January 1
- **Family Day** Third Monday in February
- **Good Friday and Easter Monday** Late March to mid-April
- **Victoria Day** Third Monday in May
- **Canada Day** July 1
- **BC Day** First Monday in August
- **Labour Day** First Monday in September
- **Thanksgiving** Second Monday in October
- **Remembrance Day** November 11
- **Christmas Day** December 25
- **Boxing Day** December 26

Safe Travel

Vancouver is relatively safe for visitors.

- Purse-snatching and pickpocketing do occur; be vigilant with your personal possessions.
- Theft from unattended cars is not uncommon; never leave valuables in vehicles where they can be seen.
- Persistent street begging is an issue for some visitors; just say 'Sorry' and pass on if you're not interested and want to be polite.
- A small group of hardcore scam artists works the downtown center, singling out tourists and asking for 'help to get back home.' Do not let them engage you in conversation.
- For the latest Covid-19 information for visitors, see hellobc.com/know-before-you-go.

Telephone

Most Vancouver-area phone numbers have the area code 604; you can also expect to see 778.

Dial all 10 digits of a given phone number, including the three-digit area code and seven-digit number, even for local calls. In some instances (eg between Vancouver and Whistler), numbers will have the same area code but will be long-distance; at such times you need to dial 1 before the area code.

Cell Phones

Local SIM cards may be used with some international phones. Roaming can be expensive: check with your service provider.

Tourist Information

The **Tourism Vancouver Visitor Center** (tourismvancouver.com) in Burrard St provides free maps, visitor guides, accommodations and tour bookings, plus brochures on the city and the wider BC region.

Visas

Not required for visitors from the US, the Commonwealth and most of Western Europe for stays up to 180 days. Visas are required by those from more than 130 other countries. However, most visa-exempt foreign nationals flying to Canada still require a $7 **Electronic Travel Authorization (eTA)**. For more information on the eTA, see canada.ca/eta. For visa information, visit the **Canada Border Services Agency** (cbsa.gc.ca) website.

Responsible Travel

Overtourism

- Visit Vancouver during less busy months such as April/May or September/October and you'll find lower accommodations costs and less crowded attractions.
- Plan days out in quieter Vancouver areas such as Kitsilano or the University of British Columbia (UBC) campus.
- Slow down and savor the wider Metro Vancouver region. Consider the North Shore for its scenic hikes and Richmond for its amazing Asian dining scene.

Lighter Footprints

- A car is not required here. Neighborhoods including Gastown, Yaletown and the West End are a short walk from downtown and are best explored on foot. Also, the public-transit system offers user-friendly services to Kitsilano, Main St, Granville Island and beyond.
- Support businesses that source locally. Shop for gifts at independent artisan stores, and buy food and produce at area farmers markets.
- Plastic shopping bags, styrofoam food containers and plastic drinking straws are banned here. Businesses also charge extra for single-use beverage cups. Plan ahead and bring your own reusable equipment.

Behind the Scenes

Send Us Your Feedback

We love to hear from travelers – your comments help make our books better. We read every word, and we guarantee that your feedback goes straight to the authors. Visit **lonelyplanet.com/contact** to submit your updates and suggestions.

Note: We may edit, reproduce and incorporate your comments in Lonely Planet products such as guidebooks, websites and digital products, so let us know if you don't want your comments reproduced or your name acknowledged. For a copy of our privacy policy visit lonelyplanet.com/privacy.

Bianca's Thanks

A heartfelt thank you to Mark, Emma, Gavin and Cloey for your patience throughout this process, and for joining me on some of my Vancouver adventures.

Love and appreciation to my parents for your unwavering support, and for raising me in the beautiful city of Vancouver.

Thank you to Grace and Heather for joining me on some of my taste-testing journeys around the city, and gratitude goes to Leila for introducing me to new restaurants in the ever-growing food scene here. To my editor Sarah Stocking, thank you for your guidance (and for answering all my questions) as we worked together to make this book possible. And thank you to John Lee for creating the previous editions of this book, which were so creative and cohesive – you made my job easier.

Acknowledgements

Cover photograph: (front) autumn, Stanley Park, romakoma/Shutterstock ©; (back) totem poles, Stanley Park, Victor Cardoner/Getty Images ©

Photographs pp34-5 (clockwise from top left) cdrin; f11photo; Noah Sauve; Bob Pool / all Shutterstock ©

This Book

This 5th edition of Lonely Planet's *Pocket Vancouver* guidebook was researched and written by Bianca Bujan. It was previously researched by John Lee. This guidebook was produced by the following:

Destination Editor
Sarah Stocking

Product Editor
Sarah Farrell

Book Designer
Dermot Hegarty

Senior Cartographer
Julie Sheridan

Coordinating Editor
Sarah Bailey

Cover Researcher
Kat Marsh

Thanks to Ronan Abayawickrema, Alison Killilea, Anne Mulvaney, Gabrielle Stefanos

Index

See also separate subindexes for:
Eating p157
Drinking p158
Entertainment p159
Shopping p159

A

accessible travel 150
accommodations 146-7
activities 24
air travel 33, 147
A-maze-ing Laughter statue 56
animals, *see* wildlife
Arbutus Greenway 141
area codes 152
art festivals 74
art galleries 26
ATMs 32, 151

B

baseball 123, 125
BC Ferries 33, 147
BC Lions 92
BC Place Stadium 89
BC Sports Hall of Fame & Museum 88
beaches
  English Bay Beach 56
  Kitsilano Beach 136
  Stanley Park Second Beach 42
  Stanley Park Third Beach 42
  Wreck Beach 133, 138
bears 124
Beaty Biodiversity Museum 136-7
beer 14
bicycling 24, 33, 149
Bill Reid Gallery of Northwest Coast Art 50
bird watching 52, 81
Birds of Raptors Ridge 61
Bloedel Conservatory 120
boat travel, *see* ferry travel
Brewery Creek 106
Burrard Bridge 82
bus travel 33, 148
business hours 150

C

Canada Day 51
Canada Place 51
cannabis 142
Capilano Suspension Bridge Park 60-1
Car Free Day 111
car hire 147
car travel 149
Carr, Emily 45
cell phones 32, 152
Ceperley Meadows 42
children, travel with 16-17, 43
Chinatown 63-77, **68**
  drinking 74-5
  entertainment 75-6
  food 70-3
  shopping 76-7
  sights 64-5, 69-70
  transportation 63
  walks 66-7, **66**
Chinatown Millennium Gate 69
Chinatown Storytelling Centre 70
Christ Church Cathedral 52
Christmas 122
City Hall 120-1
climate 146
cocktails 14
Commercial Drive 96-7, **96**
Convention Centre 47
costs 32, 150-1
coyotes 124
credit cards 151
currency 32
currency exchange 151
Cycle City Tours 53
cycling 24, 33, 149

D

disabilities, travelers with 150
Downtown 39-57, **48-9**
  drinking 54-6
  entertainment 56-7
  food 53-4
  itineraries 46-7
  shopping 57
  sights 40-5, 50-3
  transportation 39
  walks 46-7, **46**
Dr Sun Yat-Sen Classical Chinese Garden 64-5
drinking 14-15, *see also* Drinking *subindex, individual neighborhoods*
driving, *see* car travel

E

Eastside Culture Crawl 74
electricity 151
Engine 374 Pavilion 88
entertainment 20-1, *see also* Entertainment *subindex, individual neighborhoods*
Expo '86 94

Sights 000
Map Pages **000**

F

Fairmont Hotel 47
Fairview 113-27, **118-19**
drinking 123
entertainment 125
food 121-3
shopping 126-7
sights 114-15, 120-1
transportation 113
family travel 16-17, 43
farmers market 81
ferry travel 33, 147-8, 148-9
Festival of Lights 115
festivals 25, 90, 104
film festivals 20-1
food 12-13, *see also* Eating *subindex, individual neighborhoods*
food tours 82
football 89, 92
Fortes, Joe 55
Fox, Terry 89
free attractions 27

G

Gastown 63-77, **68**
architecture 70, 72
drinking 74-5
entertainment 75-6
food 70-3
shopping 76-7
sights 69-70
transportation 63
Grandview Park 97
Granville Bridge 81-2
Granville Island 79-95, **86-7**
architecture 83
drinking 91-2
entertainment 92-3
food 90-1
shopping 95
sights 80-3, 88-90
transportation 79
walks 84-5, **84**
Granville Island Brewing 89
Granville Island Public Market 80-3
Great Fire 55, 72
Greenheart TreeWalk 137-8
Grouse Mountain 17

H

Harry Jerome statue 43
highlights 6-11
hiking 24
hockey 56-7, 88
holidays 152
Hollow Tree, the 41
hotels, sustainable
Fairmont Waterfront 22-3
Shangri-La 23
HR MacMillan Space Centre 137

I

indigenous culture 43
itineraries 30-1

J

Johnson, Pauline 43

K

Ken Spencer Science Park 101
Kids Market 89
Kitsilano 129-143, **134-5**
drinking 140-1
entertainment 141
food 138-9
shopping 141-3
sights 130-1
transportation 129
Kitsilano Beach 136

L

languages 32
LGBTIQ+ travelers 28
Lonsdale Quay 59
Lord Stanley statue 43
Lost Lagoon 41
Lower Lonsdale 58-9, **58**
Lumberman's Arch 43

M

Main Street 99-111, **102**
drinking 105-9
entertainment 109
food 103-5
shopping 109-11
sights 100-1, 103
transportation 99
marijuana 142
Marine Building 50-1
maze 115
Millennium Gate 69
mobile phones 32, 152
money 32, 92, 139, 150-1
Morris & Helen Belkin Art Gallery 138
motorcycle travel 149
Museum of Anthropology 130-1
Museum of Vancouver 136
museums 26, 29

N

Nat Bailey Stadium 123
nightlife 14-15
Nitobe Memorial Garden 137
North Vancouver 58-9, **58**

O

Old Wallace Shipyards 59
Olympic Cauldron 47
Olympic Village 103
opening hours 150
outdoor activities 24

P

Pacific Central Station 33, 147
Pacific National Exhibition 108
Pacific Spirit Park 52
Polygon Gallery 59
Pride Week 28
Prospect Point 42
public holidays 152
public transportation 148-9

Q

Queen Elizabeth Park 120

R

raccoons 115, 124
Railway Foundation 94
responsible travel 22-3

Sights 000
Map Pages **000**

Richmond Night Market 13
ride share 147
Robert Burns statue 43
Roedde House Museum 29

S

safety 152
Science World 100-1
SeaBus 148
secret Vancouver 29
Shipyards District 58-9
shopping 18-19, *see also* Shopping *sub-index, individual neighborhoods*
Sins of the City Walking Tour 69-70
skunks 124
SkyTrain 148
soccer 89, 92
South Granville 113-27, **118-19**
drinking 123
entertainment 125
food 121-3
itineraries 116-17
shopping 126-7
sights 114-15, 120-1
transportation 113
walks 116-17, **116**
sports 24, 56-7, 88-9, 92-3
squirrels 124
Stanley Park 40-3, 51, 42
Stanley Park Nature House 51
Stanley Park Seawall 50
Stanley Park Train 43
Steam Clock 69

T

taxis 33, 147, 149
telephone services 32, 152
theater 20
time 32
tipping 32, 151
tourist information 152
train travel 33, 147-8
transportation 33, 147-9
Treetops Adventure 60-1

U

UBC Asian Centre 133
UBC Botanical Garden 137
University of British Columbia 129-43, **134-5**
drinking 140-1
entertainment 141
food 138-9
itineraries 132-3
shopping 141-3
sights 130-1
transportation 129
walks 132-3, **132**

V

Vancouver Aquarium 52
Vancouver Art Gallery 44-5, 47
Vancouver Biennale 56
Vancouver City Hall 120
Vancouver Convention Centre 23
Vancouver Fringe Festival 90
Vancouver International Airport 33, 147
Vancouver Maritime Museum 138
Vancouver Mural Festival 104
Vancouver Police Museum 67
Vancouver Public Library 52
Vancouver Water Adventures 90
Vancouver's oldest street 72
VanDusen Botanical Garden 114-15
Vanier Park 52
vegetarian & vegan travelers 71, 91
visas 32, 152-3

W

walking tours 22, 69-70
Chinatown Culture & History Crawl 66-7, **66**
Commercial Drive Beer & Bites 96-7, **96**
Downtown Grand Tour 46-7, **46**
Granville Island Artisan Amble 84-5, **84**
Lower Lonsdale Wander 58-9, **58**
South Granville Stroll 116-7, **116**
UBC Campus & Gardens Walk 132-3, **132**
Warren Harding statue 43
water park 43
water sports 24
weather 146
websites 23
West End 39-57, **48-9**
drinking 54-6
entertainment 56-7
food 53-4
shopping 57
sights 40-5, 50-3
transportation 39
wildlife 41-2, 61, 115, 124
wine 14
Wreck Beach 133, 138

Y

Yaletown 79-95, **86-7**
drinking 91-2
entertainment 92-3
food 90-1
history 94
shopping 95
sights 88-90
transportation 79

Eating

1931 Gallery Bistro 45

A

Acorn 104-5
Alimentaria Mexicana 90
Anh & Chi 104

B

Bao Bei 73
Blue Water Cafe 91
Boulevard Kitchen & Oyster Bar 53
Bread Affair, A 81
Burgoo 59

C

Chinatown BBQ 65
Cliff House Restaurant 61

E

Earnest Ice Cream 103-4
Elisa 71

F

Fable Diner 105
Fable Kitchen 139
Federal Store 103
Fish Counter 105
Forage 53-4

G

Go Fish 90
Granville Island Public Market 80-3

H

Havana 97
Hawksworth 54
Heirloom Vegetarian 122

J

Jam Cafe 54
Jamjar Canteen 138
Japadog 53

L

La Taquería Pinche Taco Shop 121
Lee's Donuts 85
Lift Breakfast Bakery 59
Linh Cafe 139
Lonsdale Quay Market 59
Lunch Lady 97

M

Maenam 139
Mazahr Lebanese Kitchen 123
MeeT 91
MeeT in Gastown 71

N

Naam 138-9

O

Ovaltine Cafe 70

P

Paul's Omelettery 121
Phnom Penh 70-1
Prado 97
Prospect Point Cafe 42

S

Sai Woo 71
Salmon n' Bannock 122
St Lawrence Restaurant 73
Sula Indian Restaurant 105

T

Tacofino 54
Tacofino Taco Bar 70
Tap & Barrel 105
Tojo's 122
Tony's Fish & Oyster Cafe 91
Torafuku 71
Toshi Sushi 104
Trafiq 104

U

UBC Farm Markets 131

V

Vij's 122

Y

Yasma 53

Drinking

1181 56
33 Acres Brewing 106
49th Parallel Coffee (Kitsilano) 140
49th Parallel Coffee (Main Street) 106

A

Alibi Room 74
Artisan Sake Maker 92

B

Back & Forth Bar 74-5
Botanist 55
Brassneck Brewery 105

C

Caffe Barney 123
Corduroy 141

E

East Van Brewing Company 97

F

Fountainhead Pub 55

G

Gene Cafe 107-9
Granville Island Brewing 85
Granville Island Brewing Taproom 92
Grapes & Soda 123
Guilt & Co 74

K

Keefer Bar 75
Key Party 106
Koerner's Pub 140

L

Liberty Distillery 91
Lift Bar & Grill 54-5

M

Main Street Brewing 106

N

Narrow Lounge 107

R

Revolver 74

S

Shameful Tiki | Room 106
Sing Sing Beer Bar 107
Six Acres 75
Small Victory (South Granville) 123
Small Victory (Yaletown) 91
St Augustine's 97

T

Tap & Barrel Bridges 92

U

Uva Wine & Cocktail Bar 55

Sights 000
Map Pages **000**

Entertainment

Bard on the Beach 141
BC Lions 92
Biltmore Cabaret 109
BMO Theatre Centre 109
Cinematheque 56
Commodore Ballroom 56
Firehall Arts Centre 75-6
Fox Cabaret 109
FUSE 45
Granville Island Stage 93
Khatsahlano Street Party 141
Rickshaw Theatre 75
Stanley Theatre 125
Theatre Under the Stars 56
Vancouver Canadians 125
Vancouver Canucks 56-7
Vancouver Theatresports 93
Vancouver Whitecaps 92

Shopping

Bacci's 127
Beadworks 85
Benton Brothers Fine Cheese 81
Craft Maison 97
Eastside Flea 76-7
Fine Finds 95
Front & Company 110
Garden Cafe 115
Garden Shop 115
Golden Age Collectables 57
Gore St Vintage 77
Granville Island Licorice Parlour 95
Granville Island Public Market 80-3
Granville Island Tea Company 81
Herschel Supply Co 77
Hunter & Hare 59
John Fluevog Shoes 77
Karen Cooper Gallery 95
Kasama Chocolate 85, 95
Kids Market 85
Kidsbooks 143
Kitsilano Farmers Market 141-3
Lee's Donuts 81
L'Epicerie Rotisserie & Gourmet Shop 81
Little Sister's Book & Art Emporium 57
Massy Books 76
Meinhardt Fine Foods 127
Melanie Auld 143
Mink Chocolates 57
Mintage 97
Mintage Mall 111
Mo's General Store 59
Neptoon Records 110-11
Net Loft 57
Old Faithful 143
Oyama Sausage Company 81
Pacific Arts Market 126
Paper-Ya 95
Paper Hound 57
Poppy Barley 143
Pulpfiction Books 111
Purdy's Chocolates 127
Red Cat Records 109
Regional Assembly of Text 109
Richmond Night Market 13
Siegel's Bagels 81
Stuart's Baked Goods 81
Turnabout Luxury Resale 111
UBC Farm Markets 131
Urban Source 110
Walrus 126
Zulu Records 143

Our Writer

Bianca Bujan

Born and raised in Vancouver, Bianca is an award-winning travel and food writer who loves to share the best things to see, do and eat in her home city. When traveling, Bianca enjoys connecting with cultures through cuisine and experiencing the destination through the eyes of the people who call the place home. Her work has appeared in *Lonely Planet, Food & Wine, Travel + Leisure, The Globe & Mail, Canadian Geographic, Chatelaine* and many other publications, and she has been a contributing writer for several *Lonely Planet* guidebooks and Canadian cookbooks. You can read her stories at bitsofbee.com and follow her adventures on Instagram @bitsofbee.

When she's not sharing unique travel and food experiences with her readers, Bianca enjoys spending time outdoors with her husband, three children and Dalmatian on Vancouver's North Shore, which she calls home.

Published by Lonely Planet Global Limited
CRN 554153
5th edition – Jan 2024
ISBN 978 1 83869 925 3

10 9 8 7 6 5 4 3 2 1
Printed in Malaysia